New
Pauper's
Cookbook

New
Pauper's
Cookbook

Over 250 delicious recipes
for penniless cooks

Jocasta Innes
a n d
Kate Harris

VERMILION
LONDON

For Tabitha

Published in 1992 by Vermilion
an imprint of Ebury Press
Random House UK Ltd
Random House
20 Vauxhall Bridge Road
London SW1V 2SA

A Jill Norman book

A catalogue record for this book is available from the British Library.

ISBN 0 09 175434 8

Editor: Helen Southall
Design: Bridgewater Design Ltd
Illustrator: Stewart Walton

Typeset by SX Composing Ltd, Rayleigh, Essex
Printed and bound in Great Britain by Mackays of Chatham Plc, Chatham

Contents

Introduction

The Pauper's Cookbook was first published as a paperback original in 1970, a neat little book costing 35p and promising what the blurb defined as 'good home food at Joe's Café prices'. Thanks to three minutes on BBC Radio's *World At One*, when I was quizzed by the late Bill Hardcastle about ways to cook herring, the book sold hundreds of copies in its first week, which for a cookbook by an unknown author is not bad going.

Over the next decade and a half the book was reprinted regularly. No subsequent book of mine has left such a wake of friendly feeling. Sometimes it seemed as if an entire student generation was keeping body and soul together on my Onion, Bacon and Potato Hotpot. I got thank-you letters from paupers all over the world. The potters whose casserole featured on the original cover, slightly marred by an excited drool of simulated gravy (food styling was rudimentary in those days) suddenly, two years later, presented me with its identical twin, which I still use. Even now, I am warmly greeted by strangers who swear that *The Pauper's Cookbook* fed them through the lean years scraping by on a student grant. Women have assured me, half jokingly, that it saved their marriages in the early days before they learned to cook.

The book finally petered out around the mid–Eighties; I wouldn't say that the concept had outlived its usefulness, but many of the recipes now seemed dated, or over-familiar, or downright eccentric. Besides, the book's jaunty approach to making ends meet struck something of a wrong note during the euphoric, extravagant Eighties: it seemed like a touching but irrelevant flashback to the hippy culture. I never doubted that I would get around to updating the book at some time or other, but first I had to find the right publisher, the ideal assistant, and a slot for the work. By the time this was all satisfactorily sorted out, as it happened, the boom time had evaporated and we were well into the re-cession. This gave a feeling of urgency to the project, never a bad thing. The project itself grew from a light tweaking exercise into something much more sweeping and radical. The first cut was a whole section of the original called Programmed Eating. The idea behind it – 'waste not, want not' worked through a weekly menu – was useful enough, but it felt a bit obsessive and besides we needed space for the two new sections, one on pasta, and one on vegetarian recipes, which we felt were absolutely essential in a book for a young-ish readership in the Nineties. Next, I went through the original text crossing out all the recipes that struck me as out of date, something which is easier to recognise than to define. A lot of 'so-what' recipes went too. A 'so-what' recipe is one that would be okay if you could be bothered to make it – but mostly you can't. What remained after this bracing surgery was a core of workable, economical recipes that had worn well, classics you might say, but from many different cuisines, Chinese, Indian, Russian, Greek and North African as well as traditional British. None of my readers' favourites was struck off. The famous Onion, Bacon and Potato Hotpot is still there but has been joined by many more hotpots, one-dish meals which we favour. We have put back rather more recipes than we took out, but what is more to the point, the new recipes are altogether superior, more varied, more authoritative and more reliable. This is not an idle boast: nor is it so surprising, really. My cooking has improved over 20 years, but food standards in general have risen dramatically and our book reflects this. People today eat a much healthier, more interesting diet than they did then, and they cook and shop with an open-mindedness that owes a great deal to the foodie cults that have come and, in some cases, gone; to the improvement in restaurant standards; to the wider choice of ingredients available; and last, but not least, to the cooking they grew up with, the 'good home food' of my 1970 blurb.

After much discussion, we decided to keep to the original format where recipes were grouped into situations (Fast Work is an obvious example) rather than generically, ie soups, eggs, fish and so on. I hope the headings explain themselves, but for new readers here is a short breakdown of the sections:

STANDARDS: Everyday dishes one does not tire of, on the substantial side, with an emphasis on one-pot meals, including recipes for everything from soups to puds.

PADDING: Basic know-how and some recipes for stretching more expensive ingredients with cheap, useful staples – rice, batter, pulses, grains, etc.

FAST WORK: The emphasis on speed, with some reliance on store-cupboard items and the freezer.

PASTA FASTER: No spag bol (well, you know that one already) but some corkers, simple, sophisticated and sophisticatedly simple.

8

VEGGIES: Non-meat and non-fish eaters (not vegans, however) should find this a mini-cookbook, going through from soups and salads to solid dishes and party food.

FANCY WORK: Recipes for special occasions. They may cost a bit more, take a bit longer, or introduce exotica. Paupers, especially, need to splurge occasionally; these dishes let you splurge safely.

PRIVATE ENTERPRISE: Extras like home-made preserves, bread and mayonnaise add a welcome dash of luxury to a scrimping budget. They may also be cheaper than the bought kind.

One innovation we thought up is a trio of simple visual symbols. There are lots of instances in a book like this where recipes could go under several different headings. Most pasta dishes, for instance, are quick to make but we put them in Pasta Faster rather than in Fast Work. Likewise there are many veggie dishes outside the veggie chapter, as well as in it. The symbols adopted are explained below. 'Vegetarian' and 'Quick', by the way, are not used in Veggies and Fast Work for obvious reasons and we did not think it was useful to mark vegetarian desserts and sweet things.

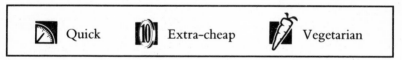

I am no longer a pauper, though with all my capital tied up in my own small business, I can hardly afford complacency. However, I still cook the sort of food we advocate in this book, because it is the sort of food we like in my household, simple but varied, cheap but gutsy. Young Kate, my co-author, cooks imaginatively on the sort of budget I juggled with 20 years ago, and she monitored my recipes for unacceptable extravagances as well as to bridge any generation gaps. I have dedicated this book to my daughter, Tabitha, whose birth more or less coincided with its first appearance. I had hoped it might be out in time to be useful during her last university year: instead she made do with the old version. I am told that this bright but scatty girl of mine cooks really well, when she puts her mind to it. If she can do it – and with this thought I leave you – there is hope for you all.

JOCASTA INNES

Where the Money Goes

Indisputably, it goes. But it is possible to control the outflow and see that you get value for your money. Sensible shopping, the domestic equivalent of a planned economy, does save actual money, largely by cutting down on wastage, and it should also ensure that you have good quality materials to cook with.

Without going to the lengths of keeping itemized accounts of everything you spend, you will need to introduce a little system into your shopping, to avoid fetching up broke and hungry half-way through the week. The first thing is to decide how much you want, or can afford, to spend on food each week. Make a rough estimate of your weekly consumption of essentials like bread, butter, eggs, tea, milk, and what this costs. Subtract the figure from your weekly budget, divide the remainder by seven, and you are left with a pretty good idea of what your daily expenditure should be. If you keep well within this figure for half the week, you will have accumulated enough to buy something special for the weekend, or stock up on cans, extra herbs, sauces, etc.

A shopping list is the most effective curb on over-stepping your daily food budget. Decide what you are going to eat, check the recipe against what you have already got, list what you need, and *stick* to the list. Elementary, I know, but for every steel-trap mind there must be ten impulse buyers bumbling round the shops, trusting to association of ideas to come up with the right answers. A fallible system at any time, and positively dangerous in supermarkets. On the other hand, don't become too inflexible – if a good buy crops up unexpectedly, cheap pheasant, say, or herrings, you should be able to revise your other purchases accordingly. A little homework with this cookbook ought to help there.

The foregoing three paragraphs, written 20 years ago, still seem to me sensible advice. I still shop around for shops, though like most busy people living in a big city I tend to do one massive weekly session at the nearest supermarket for boring basics.

For the rest, I supplement these with sorties to specialist shops, markets, farm shops, foodie boutiques, church fêtes. There is a sameness about supermarket food: one can live with it, or off it, but sometimes paupers need a bit of the genuine article, the taste, the smell, even, of excellence. This means more to people hemmed in by cash restrictions than to fat cats. I journey to Islington for fresh fish. Meat I buy from a family butcher, who also sells game. Lamb/mutton I buy from a local hallal butcher. Home-made sausages come from a farm shop in Essex, where my mother lives. I shop in markets, in London or the country, whenever I can; markets often have excellent fish, seafood, cheeses, preserves and local produce. London's first 'all organic' market, by the way, selling meat, fruit, vegetables and wholefoods, has recently opened in Spitalfields, on the site of the old fruit and vegetable market. I always end up lugging some food treasure back from trips abroad – olive oil, air-cured ham, salami, strings of garlic, Tunisian spices. Does this sound like a lot of trouble to go to? I enjoy the discoveries, which add a point to so many trips, here and abroad. Some of these things are luxuries, but there is a trade-off: the money I save *not* buying packaged sauces, frozen dinners, tubes of garlic purée, bottled mayonnaise and so on ad infinitum (convenience foods, in a word) seems prudently invested on such items as free-range eggs, fine tea and organic vegetables.

Shops

Before deciding which shops to patronise, compare prices and the range and quality of goods on display. The butcher for you is one who stocks a wide range of good-quality cheap cuts as well as offal, rabbit and pigeons. Your fishmonger should offer bargains like mussels, fresh herring and sprats in season. Your greengrocer ought to stock a selection of local produce (this applies less to large towns of course) as well as imported stuff. Where two shops are much of a muchness, go for the one with the friendlier staff. Having made your choice, try and stick to it. Shopkeepers take more trouble over their regulars.

Paupers, my mother crisply observed, cannot afford to be squeamish, and she has a point. Don't be cowardly about trying something new, odd, or unprepossessing-looking. Most shoppers go for the obvious, safe and familiar, particularly in the meat line – chops and frying steak, according to my butcher – with the result that these get pricier while offbeat items are often absurdly cheap. The less snob cuts of meat like shin of beef, hand of pork, many varieties of game, and most of what goes under the unfortunate name of 'offal' – kidneys, liver, etc. – are all good buys and make good eating when properly

11

cooked. In the fish line, try mussels, sprats, coley and bream as well as mackerel and herring. I often find humble vegetables like kale and spring greens more rewarding, carefully cooked, than more expensive foreign imports.

Planning

My food planning for the week is definitely broad brush; I buy one good-sized chicken, a pound or so of smoked fish, and a ring of smoked sausage, regularly. These, plus any leftovers and by-products (chicken stock, haddock stock), and padded out with potatoes, grains, pulses or whatever, will see us through four or five meals. On Sundays we get large packs of fresh mussels (the new food of the poor, with frozen chicken livers) to eat first as soup, then with pasta. I usually have smoked salmon and bacon scraps in the fridge. Both are versatile, and a little goes a long way. I am lucky in having a box of organic veg delivered once a week, nine months of the year. These spoil fast so I have to rush into action; we have lots of cooked salads (beets, turnips, broad beans) as well as raw ones. I make gratins, ratatouille, purées to freeze for soups later, impromptu salade niçoise combinations to eat with hard-boiled eggs, canned tuna and aïoli. We eat meat less often than we used to, preferring game in season. If I buy pork I salt it over-night (just rub in salt well all over) to leach out some of that sinister moisture it seems to be pumped with; I find this, *pace* Jane Grigson, improves taste and texture. Every time I finish a book I promise myself to take up bread-making again, using Fleur's recipe (see page 180), because my family eat bread like it was just invented and home-made bread is such a luxury. Here is a list of thrifty buys, little altered since 1970.

OLIVE OIL : Buy the largest size you can afford of the strongest tasting oil (usually green, from Cyprus, Greece or Spain). It is now accepted as healthier than butter or margarine for cooking, and it is nicer than the other vegetable oils. You can extend it with safflower or sunflower oil.

RICE : Asian cash-and-carries sell whopping bags of patna or basmati rice, at a price that works out markedly cheaper. Rice keeps well, stored in a mouse-proof bin. Or you could go shares with friends. Uncle Ben's Long-Grain Rice can replace Italian arborio for risotto. Brown rice is good for salads.

SPICES: It's daft to buy all your spices in those titchy jars in super-markets. Get black peppercorns, coriander seeds and cumin in 500 g (1 lb) packs from Asian supermarkets, likewise ground turmeric, ginger and garam masala. The best value saffron is powdered, in sachets, from Italian and Spanish delis. Use fresh chillies sometimes in-stead of dried; they are high in Vitamin C, and smell ineffably fresh, like cucumber but more so.

SPECIALITY STORES: Get your Chinese sauces, seasonings, wonton wrappers, etc., from a Chinese foodstore. Healthfood stores tend to be pricy, but may be the only source of unusual items like dried seaweed, laver bread, buckwheat, brown lentils, agar–agar and millet.

TEA: Teabag tea tastes like dust to me. I buy packets of favourite oriental blends, like Lapsang, and mix them with cheaper but not rub-bishy standard blends, for their fragrance.

BACON/GAMMON: Supermarkets have taken to selling packs of off-cuts of bacon and gammon which one can do a lot with in a pauper kitchen. A bonus is, quite often, that the meat itself seems rather better quality, not so watery. Trim pieces into neat chunks or strips and cook as usual.

BITS AND BONES: Get to know a family butcher, and a good fishmonger and charm them into giving you marrow bones, fresh suet, caul fat, pigs' trotters, odd white fish heads, bones and trimmings for stock.

PULSES, GRAINS, ETC: Best bought in moderate size bags (1–2 kg/2¼–4½ lb) from wholefood or healthfood shops. These dete-riorate more rapidly than rice, on the whole, so go for a store with a rapid turnover.

HERBS: You can get seedlings everywhere nowadays, potted up. Basil, thyme, chives and parsley grow well for me in windowboxes or large tubs, in a sunny place. Dill grows like a weed in the ground, as does fennel.

CRÈME FRAÎCHE: Mix yogurt with fresh cream and leave overnight to develop that faint refreshing acidity characteristic of crème fraîche.

P A S T A : Forget the so-called 'fresh' pasta, unless from an Italian deli; it is floppy and tasteless. Get a good brand of dried durum wheat pasta, cheaper and nicer. And try making your own (see page 99).

Stocking Up

The following is a list of useful things to have by at all times and especially for the Fast Work recipes in this book. No need to rush out and buy them all at once; the most useful are in italics.

C A N S : Tuna, *anchovies*, corned beef, *peeled tomatoes, tomato purée.*

F R O Z E N F O O D S : *peas, broad beans, sweetcorn, chicken livers.*

S A U C E S / C O N D I M E N T S : *dry mustard, Dijon mustard, soy sauce* (Japanese brands are best), Worcestershire sauce, Tabasco, *white wine vinegar*, honey, molasses.

P U L S E S / G R A I N S / C E R E A L S : *green and brown lentils, chickpeas*, flageolets, barley, buckwheat, burghul, couscous, channa dal, *polenta, strong white bread flour*, cornflour, easy-cook long-grain rice (or arborio), *brown rice*.

S P I C E S : buy in small quantities – *juniper berries*, allspice, cinnamon sticks, vanilla pods, *whole nutmegs*.

D R I E D F R U I T : *raisins, sultanas*, prunes, dates, apricots.

V A N I L L A S U G A R : This improves most puddings, cakes and biscuits, used in place of ordinary granulated or caster sugar. You can make your own very easily by buying a few vanilla pods from a good grocer or delicatessen and storing them in a covered jar or tin of caster sugar. The vanilla pods can be used for flavouring milk puddings and custards, rinsed, dried and put back in the jar. They can be used three or four times.

O P T I O N A L E X T R A S : capers, *olives*, dried tomatoes, oyster sauce, *black bean sauce, dried red chillies*, bitter chocolate, pine nuts.

You will also need a supply of *lemons* (a pauper's answer to wine marinades), peanut oil for deep frying, *garlic, fresh ginger*, breadcrumbs (home-made from stale bread dried in the oven and pounded), fast-action yeast in packets. Use Parmesan or Pecorino where it matters, bought in a chunk and grated, although Cheddar or a sharper hard cheese can be substituted – Lancashire, Cheshire, mature Gouda, etc.

Wherewithal

Improvisation is the key-word here. Paupers are often pushed for space as well as cash and the logical answer is to have a minimum of equipment, which can double up for different purposes.

STORAGE: Simplest, cheapest and handiest way of keeping it out of the way when not in use is to borrow a practical French trick and hang as much as possible from hooks, or plain nails, in the walls.

If you are short of working surfaces, and your kitchen space can accommodate another piece of furniture, look for a low cupboard (waist-height, or lower) in a junk shop. Cover it with formica, or a slab of marble off an old washstand – the latter makes the ideal pastry board. The cupboard will take casseroles, etc., and groceries. Fifties utility kitchen units are good for storage.

WHERE TO BUY: Junk shops, Oxfam shops and boot sales are fruitful locales for kitchen equipment. For once the consumer society works in your favour. Households which have gone mad for stainless steel, and enamelled cast-iron, often throw out a mass of serviceable pots, pans and utensils. Dingy to look at, perhaps, but often surprisingly good quality. Weight is a reliable indication of quality – the heavier your saucepan or casserole, the better it holds and diffuses heat.

Look out for: aluminium pans and stoneware casseroles, the latter usually brown or green outside, cream within. They often arrive lidless, but inverted plates or foil will substitute in most cases. You can't have too many china mixing bowls – a 'slight fault' doesn't matter if you don't bash it too heartily. Glass storage jars (must have tops) and canisters are useful for storing perishable foods. Bread boards, rolling pins, carving knives, are all worth looking out for. Antiquated gadgets, if you can work out what they are *for*, are often good buys and usually work very efficiently with a little cleaning and oiling.

For anything else, try a good ironmongers.

WHAT YOU WILL NEED: The following is a skeleton selection of equipment but it should prove adequate for the recipes in this book. Again, there is no need to buy all of it at once – keep adding to it as occasion arises and cash permits.

COOK'S KNIFE: One thing you cannot do without. It should be medium size, sharp as a razor, and good quality. You need it for slicing and trimming meat, chopping vegetables, herbs, peeling potatoes, de-rinding bacon, and a host of other jobs. Quality pays off here. If you can't wangle one as a present, save up, and in the meantime hunt up an old-fashioned non-stainless kitchen knife in a junk shop and sharpen it regularly on a carborundum. Stainless, serrated-edged knives are adequate for peeling and scraping vegetables.

SWIVEL-BLADED PEELER: A tiny but invaluable gadget for paring carrots, etc., as well as for peeling spuds.

CHOPPING BOARD: Essential. The back of a wooden bread board will do. Scrub it often or garlic will permeate everything.

SAUCEPANS: Two is the minimum. One medium-to-large, one a size or two smaller. The big one for soups, pasta, rice, which need a lot of liquid; the smaller one for vegetables, etc. You can improvise a double boiler by standing the smaller pan inside the larger one. A very small pan is best for boiling eggs, milk, sauces.

CASSEROLES: Two again. Big one for stews, pot roasts and bulky dishes. Smaller for milk pudding, pâtés, soufflés, fish pie, etc. I find stoneware the most versatile material for the money.

SIEVE: A fairly capacious one for sieving, or puréeing soup, sauces, stewed fruit, flour. Metal is strongest, good quality plastic adequate, as long as you don't hold it over direct heat. You need a nylon sieve for sieving acidic fruit.

COLANDER: People muddle along without, by juggling with saucepan lids or plates, but colanders save time and scalds and you can pick them up cheaply in junk shops – the metal ones are better than your plastics, as they don't melt.

FRYING PAN: One medium-sized one will cope with most frying jobs. It should be a heavyweight one, but the lighter kind is adequate if you use it with a heat diffuser mat to prevent food sticking and burning. A non-stick one is brilliant for pancakes, frittata, tortilla.

ROASTING PAN: The cheapest is all right. A medium-sized pan will take shepherd's pie and upside-down puddings, as well as roasts.

GRILL PAN: Some elderly cookers have lost their grill pans. You need one, though, for grilling meat, as well as toasting bread.

MIXING BOWLS: One sturdy, large one for mixing batters, etc. A small one for beating up egg whites, mayonnaise. But you can always do with more, so keep your eyes open.

FLAN TIN: One 20 or 23 cm (8 or 9 inch) tin is essential. Better still, two, so you can bake two pastry cases at once, storing the extra one in an airtight tin.

MEASURING JUG: I have a large plastic beaker which cost a few pence. It gives fluid ml/oz, litre/pint, sugar and flour measurement tables separately, and I find it invaluable. Kitchen scales are not so vital because exact measurements are less important with bulky dishes, but for pastry and cake making, where accuracy matters, the beaker is essential.

IMPLEMENTS: You will need two or three wooden spoons, a metal spatula for lifting fried foods, an egg whisk, a coffee strainer and a grater. The last is essential for grating cheese, lemon rind, vegetables, and worth every penny it costs. Best are the four-sided plastic graters – stable and less painful on the knuckles.

When you can add to this basic selection, you should concentrate first on extra saucepans and casseroles. Other useful oddments are a loaf tin, good for baking Meat Loaf, Caramel Custards and cakes; a shallow ovenproof dish for baking fish and vegetables, or milk puddings; a garlic press (chefs swat the bulb with a heavy chopper but, in less skilful hands, the fragments tend to fly round the room).

If you have an odd pound to spare any time, a mouli food mill is a gadget to invest in. Childishly simple to use, it takes the slog out of mushing soup, fruit and vegetables. But, of course, if you can persuade a parent or relative to pass on their superannuated food processor, you are laughing. These can be serviced and new blades obtained.

One last aid to cooking without tears. Free too! When making mayonnaise, put the oil in a corked bottle with a deep notch cut in one side of the cork. This regulates the flow of oil, greatly simplifying the task of adding it drop by drop to the egg (see page 170).

Rules of Thumb

Not surprisingly, pauper kitchens tend to be light on equipment. When money is tight, one spends it on food rather than kitchen scales, sets of mixing bowls or measuring spoons. Bearing this in mind, there are few recipes, if any, in this book where quantities or timing are critical. Relative proportions – rather than hairs' breadth accuracy – are important in making a béchamel sauce, soufflés or cakes. Timing obviously counts when roasting meat or cooking soufflés and such items as pasta and rice. Largely, though, cooking successfully is a matter of commonsense. If you are short of meat for a casserole, bung in more vegetables, slices of garlic sausage, pulses, barley, dumplings, etc. etc. If one ingredient in a list is missing, you can often do without, or substitute another, without wrecking the outcome. Again, use your loaf about this. Onion soup cannot be made without onions, or bread without flour (though this doesn't have to be wheat flour) but chicken recipes also suit rabbit, and vice versa; swedes or parsnips can supply the sweetness of carrots in soups and stews; Worcestershire sauce can stand in, at a pinch, for soy sauce; nutmeg can be used instead of cinnamon or cloves; and many herbs are interchangeable. The dish will be different with different ingredients, but you might even prefer it that way, *your* way.

The following tips and suggestions are dedicated to making cooking feel relaxed, not frantic.

Quantities

- 1 level teaspoon = 5 ml
- 1 level tablespoon = 15 ml

As a rough but useful guide, the following tablespoon quantities yield 25 g (1 oz):

Butter/margarine – 2 level tablespoons
Caster sugar – 2 level tablespoons
Uncooked rice – 2 level tablespoons
Unsifted flour – 3 level tablespoons

- 1 glass = approximately 175 ml (6 fl oz)
- 1 tea-cup = approximately 150 ml (¼ pint)

A plastic measuring jug or beaker, with quantities marked off on the

18

sides, will see you through most recipes. Use it to weigh out sugar, flour and rice as well as liquids. Failing this, many foods you buy have their weight marked on them – a quarter of a standard butter pack weighs 50 g (2 oz), for example. And it may seem crashingly obvious, but I will still mention that a milk bottle equals 568 ml (1 pint).

In estimating serving quantities, I work on the following per person (these are approximate and a little on the stingy side):

- For pasta and rice – 75-125 g (3-4 oz)
- Other pulses and grains – 75 g (3 oz)
- Meat and fish – 125 g (4 oz)

Timing

MEAT AND POULTRY: The basic rule for roasting meat and poultry is to give it 20 minutes per 450 g (1 lb) and a further 20 minutes 'for the pot'. Pork should be cooked for 30 minutes per 450 g (1 lb) plus 30 minutes. Braising and boiling times are the same. Remember to check the weight before you throw the wrapping away.

To check that poultry is cooked, insert a knife in the fleshy part where the leg joins the body – the juices should run clear.

FISH: Fish is delicate stuff. If you are baking it in foil or in a dish, put it in the centre of a preheated oven at 180°C (350°F) mark 4, and allow 8 minutes per 450 g (1 lb) for a whole fish, plus 10 minutes, and 10–20 minutes in total for fillets and steaks.

To check that fish is cooked, insert a knife near the backbone – again, the juices should run clear.

All roast meats and fish are best if left to 'rest' in a warm place for 10-20 minutes before serving – which gives you a bit of leeway in timing your meal.

RICE: White, long-grain rice should be boiled fast in lots of salted water for 12 minutes, then rinsed and dried off in a low oven. Cooking times for brown rice vary – it usually takes upwards of 40 minutes.

PASTA: With dried pasta, check the makers' instructions, but start testing it *sooner* rather than later. 'Fresh', but especially home-made, pasta cooks in a much shorter time – test after 2 minutes.

Standards

All the recipes in this chapter come into a category unrecognised, so far as I know, by cooking literature, but familiar to every reasonably experienced cook who usually makes his or her personal selection as time goes by. Quite simply, these are dishes which one can, and does, go back to, over and over again, with renewed pleasure and appetite. They extend over the whole field of eating – soups, salads, main dishes, puddings. They must taste good, certainly, in a homely rather than subtle fashion. They are often, though not always, easy to make successfully. Their components tend to be straight-forward, and associative as well – pork and beans, frankfurters and red cabbage – which makes the shopping easier, especially from memory. They are, of course, thrifty, but without appearing stingy. Still, in the last resort, their appeal is elusive, and just why one should keep returning to these, after many promising alternatives have been discarded, is something of a mystery.

There is nothing mysterious, however, about my reason for choosing to start my book with a whole collection of cooking Standards. I am convinced, from analysing my own experience and the food offered up regularly by friends, family and acquaintances, that these are the most useful recipes for an inexperienced cook to start on, a good foundation on which to build a more elaborate repertoire as experience and confidence grow. Once you have mastered a selection of these recipes, you will be able to feed yourself and others cheaply, efficiently and well, and you will have picked up some useful knowledge along the way.

A few specific points:

SOUPS: Ideal pauper's food – cheap, nourishing and good for you. If your experience is limited to canned or packet varieties, you have no idea how good soup can be. A solid minestrone, with grated cheese, or a French onion soup poured over slices of bread, is almost a meal in itself. Certainly a light lunch. A lighter vegetable soup is, say, half a meal, and should be rounded out with a light main dish – grilled fish, pâté and salad, or an omelette.

MAIN DISHES: Most in this chapter are substantial and need no more than one vegetable dish or salad as accompaniment. Many have their own stodge built in. Leftovers can be warmed up – indeed many of these dishes improve with keeping, within reason.

PUDDINGS: Fresh fruit addicts probably won't bother with these. All the same it is worth learning up a few because they are useful when you have a lot of people to feed. Children love them, and so, oddly enough, do most men. A simple sweet like Bread and Butter Pudding rounds off a skimpy meal pleasantly.

A guiding rule is that a meal can either be built round one solid dish, needing very little with, before or after, or a succession of lightweight dishes. The first is less trouble, the second offers more variety and is a better summer formula when salads and fruit are cheap and plentiful.

Simple Stock

What might be called serious stock-making, involving long cooking of selected meats and bones, plus clarifying with egg white, belongs today to the world of professional cheffery. However, any domestic cooking, and pauper meals especially, benefits enormously from the enriching properties of an easily made bowl of simple stock that can be kept in the fridge for several days, and used as the basis of soups, sauces, casserole dishes and much else. I tend to cook chicken, or one of the game birds in season (pheasant is sometimes as cheap as chicken) once a week, knowing that it will not only provide two meals, at a pinch, but also a supply of fresh, versatile stock to build into the week's meals.

I apply the same method, if anything so rough and ready can be called a method, to the remains of whatever bird we have eaten. Collect up all the bones, plus the carcass, plus any jellied cooking juices or congealed gravy, then chop them all across with a cleaver (to release the bone marrow), and dump the lot in a casserole with cold water to cover. Cover and cook in the oven at 140°C (275°F) mark 1 for several hours to extract whatever flavour and richness remains. What starts off as an unappetising-looking panful of skin, scraps and bones (I mention this because too often people chuck these useful remnants away simply because they look so grungy) gradually yields up a quantity of lightly coloured, potentially savoury, broth with manifold uses.

Strain off the debris, leave the stock to cool in a bowl, then store in the fridge. This, as it is, will enormously enhance soups, pasta sauces, etc., 'rounding out' their essential flavours. A good simple stock sets to a light jelly with a layer of fat on top which can be scraped off and used to fry potatoes or croûtons.

Two points should be noted about this simple stock: It should not be seasoned at this stage, because any salting and peppering will become exaggerated during further reducing, and if it contains any vegetable ingredients, such as onions, herbs, stuffing, etc., it will need boiling up for a few minutes every few days (every 48 hours to be on the safe side) to prevent it souring and spoiling.

Simple Fish Stock

Most fish dishes are improved by the addition of fish stock, which intensifies the flavour markedly – whether you are making a fish soup, prawn curry, baking whole fish, or looking for the makings of a simple sauce to accompany poached, grilled or baked fish. This need not be a performance. For instance, if you make a point of buying prawns in their shells, it is no great bother to cook up the shells with water to cover and maybe a few chopped spring onions, for 20–30 minutes. This is more trouble than reaching for a packet of frozen shelled prawns, I agree, but the payoff in terms of taste is seriously interesting. Not everyone realises how much fishy taste there is in prawn shells, not to mention other fishy debris, such as bones, skin and fish heads. I doubt that many paupers are so organised they cook up a regular supply of fish stock, to freeze, just in case, but any time you are contemplating a big fish dish, for a party perhaps, it is commonsense to grab whatever 'bits' are available (a wise fishmonger will always let you have odds and ends, for a pittance, that would otherwise be thrown away) and cook the lot up for stock. Fresh fish is exquisite food, worth taking a little or even a *lot* more trouble over.

The fish trimmings to use for stock are best taken from so-called white fish, ie non-oily, fish. Oily fish – mackerel, herring, fresh sardines – have too pronounced a flavour, which when reduced down overpowers everything else. In this sense, fish stock should be neutral, but *fishy*. The making is simplicity itself. Put all the 'bits' into a large pan, including any prawn shells if you have them, cover with cold water, and bring very slowly to the boil. Skim off any scum that rises, reduce the heat and simmer for about 30 minutes. Strain off the liquid. Reduce by further simmering, uncovered, for another 10-15 minutes or until the broth begins to waft a marine tang, and looks less watery and a little more coloured. This is now the ideal liquid to add to any of the above-mentioned dishes, either solo or sharpened with wine, cider, a drop of wine vinegar or lemon juice. Keep the initial stock as plain as possible if you plan to freeze it or keep it in the fridge. It is the vegetable or herb additions which turn stock sour faster. And skip the salt and pepper, too, because reduction strengthens these flavours undesirably.

French Onion Soup

4 SERVINGS

a knob of butter
4 large or 6 small onions, thickly
    sliced
1.1 litres (2 pints) Simple Stock (see
    page 21)

salt and pepper
4 thick slices of bread
125 g (4 oz) Cheddar cheese, grated

Melt the butter in a heavy-based saucepan and fry the onions over a moderate heat until golden brown. Stir from time to time to prevent them sticking. Pour in the stock and bring to the boil, then reduce the heat, cover and simmer for 30-45 minutes. Taste and season.

Toast the slices of bread and remove the crusts if you are fussy. Serve the soup in individual bowls. Float a slice of toast on each serving and sprinkle generously with grated cheese.

Artichoke Soup

This soup is made with Jerusalem artichokes, which look like small knobbly potatoes, not the leafy globe variety. Artichokes have a pronounced, though delicate, flavour, which makes a very good soup.

4 SERVINGS

450 g (1 lb) Jerusalem artichokes
25 g (1 oz) butter
900 ml (1½ pints) water and 1 stock
   cube, or 900 ml (1½ pints)
   Simple Stock (see page 21)

salt and pepper
freshly grated nutmeg
a little single cream

Peel and slice the artichokes, then heat them gently in the butter for a few minutes. Add the water and stock cube, or Simple Stock, making sure the artichokes are covered by about 2.5 cm (1 inch). Season with salt, pepper and nutmeg, bring to the boil, then reduce the heat and simmer gently for 45 minutes–1 hour or until the artichokes are tender.

Press the soup through a sieve into a bowl, then return it to the pan and add a little cream. Heat through gently before serving.

If you have time, make some croûtons (see page 29) to eat with this. The small cubed sort are best, sprinkled over the soup.

Celery Soup

An excellent, easily made soup, which really tastes of the vegetable.

4-6 SERVINGS

a knob of butter
1 small head of celery, trimmed and
   roughly chopped (leaves included)
1 large potato, peeled and chopped
1.1 litres (2 pints) stock, or 600 ml
   (1 pint) stock and 600 ml (1 pint)
   milk

salt and pepper
freshly grated nutmeg
a little butter, to serve (optional)

Melt the butter in a large saucepan and gently stew the vegetables in it until well coated. This preliminary stew-frying of the vegetables makes the soup richer and tastier.

24

Add the stock, bring to the boil, cover the pan and cook steadily for 45 minutes, or until the celery is soft. It needs to be soft because you have to press it through a sieve.

After sieving, return the soup to the pan, add the milk now if you are using milk, stir well and heat through. Taste, and add salt and pepper and a little grated nutmeg. Just before serving, you can stir in a little butter. Croûtons (see page 29) go well with this.

Minestrone

More a meal than a soup, this is economical, because only the greediest people would demand more than an omelette to follow. You can play about with the ingredients according to what is at hand, adding odd scraps of boiled bacon, a bacon bone, and such vegetables as are cheap and in season, but keep to the rule of putting slow-cooking vegetables in ahead of the quicker cooking ones. Other vegetables which can go in include celery, beans, peas, a Jerusalem artichoke or two, even a few spring greens, well trimmed. Of course, using Simple Stock (see page 21) instead of water and stock cubes gives a much richer soup.

4-6 SERVINGS

1 tablespoon vegetable oil
125 g (4 oz) belly of pork or bacon
    rashers, de-rinded and chopped
3 onions, sliced
3 garlic cloves, sliced
1.7 litres (3 pints) hot stock
125 g (4 oz) dried haricot beans,
    soaked overnight and drained
1 bay leaf
a pinch of dried thyme
a pinch of dried marjoram

227 g (8 oz) can tomatoes, or
    2 tablespoons tomato purée
3 carrots, sliced
1 turnip, sliced
2-3 potatoes, peeled and sliced
½ small cabbage, shredded
1 leek, sliced (optional)
a handful of small pasta shapes
salt and pepper
grated Parmesan or Pecorino cheese,
    to serve

Heat the oil in a large saucepan and gently fry the belly of pork or bacon, onions and garlic, stirring to make sure nothing burns. Add the hot stock, haricot beans, bay leaf, thyme and marjoram, and the tomatoes or tomato purée. Boil for 1½-2 hours, or until tender.

Add the carrots, turnip and potatoes to the soup. Ten minutes later put in the cabbage, leek (if using) and the pasta. After a further 10 minutes, taste, and add salt and pepper as needed.

Serve this soup with a bowl of grated Parmesan cheese so everyone can help themselves, and large slices of bread and butter.

25

Borshch

Borshch is to Russia what Scotch Broth is to Scotland. It is a cheering soup to look at, ruby red, and the beetroot and soured cream give it an interesting acidulated sweetness.

If you have any pickled beetroot, 1 tablespoon of the juice can be added to the borshch. The soup can be made equally successfully with vegetable stock.

4-6 SERVINGS

1.1 litres (2 pints) Simple Stock (see page 21)
450 g (1 lb) uncooked beetroot, peeled and diced
1 onion, roughly chopped
1 carrot, roughly chopped
salt and pepper
150 ml (¼ pint) soured cream

Put the stock in a large saucepan, add the vegetables and bring to the boil, then reduce the heat, cover and simmer for 1–2 hours or until the beetroot is very pale and the soup very red. Add salt and pepper.

The Russian way would be to strain off the vegetables, but if you prefer a thicker soup you could sieve them and return them to the pan. A spoonful of soured cream is added to each helping of soup.

Smoked Haddock Chowder

The basis for this comforting and filling soup is the milk which has been used to cook just a small amount of smoked haddock. The milk leaches out a surprisingly strong, smoky taste, which you can reinforce with the reserved fish and a few mussels or prawns. But the basis remains the combination of flavoured milk, potatoes and onion.

4 SERVINGS

smoked haddock fillet
568-900 ml (1-1½ pints) milk
1 tablespoon vegetable oil
25 g (1 oz) butter
2-3 medium-sized onions, finely chopped
4 medium-sized potatoes, peeled and diced
salt and black pepper
freshly grated nutmeg
1-2 tablespoons cooked mussels (see page 27), shells removed, or peeled prawns, or a mixture
1 tablespoon finely chopped fresh parsley

Put the haddock fillet in a shallow pan or flameproof baking dish, cover with milk, bring to a simmer and simmer gently for 15–20 minutes. Drain off the milk and reserve it. Flake the fish, removing any skin and bones.

Heat the oil and butter over a medium heat in a heavy-based saucepan, and, when hot, add the onions and potatoes. Give the pan a good shake to coat the contents in the buttery oil. Turn the heat down, cover the pan and leave to sweat over a low heat until the onion is transparent. Pour over the reserved milk, adding a little water to cover the ingredients, if necessary (this is a solid sort of soup). Re-cover the pan and cook gently for about 10 minutes or until the potato is tender. Season to taste with salt, pepper and nutmeg, add the fish and shellfish, and heat through over a low heat for a few minutes. Ladle into shallow soup plates, sprinkle with parsley and serve.

Moules MacCormac

This excellent dish began life as moules marinières with knobs on, acquired an Asian fillip under the tutelage of cookery writer Daramjit Singh, plus modifications suggested by an exceptional mussel broth in Edinburgh, and was then surprised to find its twin in a medieval dish described in Dorothy Hartley's *Food in England*. Whatever its pedigree, it is always worth waiting for.

6-8 SERVINGS

900 g (2 lb) fresh mussels	1 teaspoon ground turmeric, or
50 g (2 oz) butter	½ teaspoon saffron threads
450 g (1 lb) onions, chopped	a pinch of cayenne pepper
2 large leeks, chopped	salt and black pepper
2 garlic cloves, chopped	300 ml (½ pint) dry white wine
1 cm (½ inch) cube of fresh root	200 ml (7 fl oz) cream (optional)
ginger, peeled and chopped	a small handful of fresh parsley or
125 ml (4 fl oz) water	coriander, finely chopped

Put the mussels in clean water and scrub them well. Pull and scrape off the beards and any barnacles with a small stout knife. Any mussels that are not tightly closed, or feel unusually heavy (which can mean a shell full of mud), should be discarded. Leave the mussels in cold water while you prepare the vegetable base for the soup.

Melt the butter in a large heavy-based saucepan with a lid and soften the onions and leeks over moderate heat, with the lid half on. Add the garlic and ginger and leave to simmer, without browning.

Drain the mussels and put them in a large pan with the water. Cook over a high heat and shake and turn them with a wooden spoon for 1-2 minutes or until they are all open. Remove immediately. (Discard any mussels that remain stubbornly closed.) The mussels should be just

27

firm enough to remove from the shells. Using a slotted spoon, lift the mussels out on to a large dish and cool slightly.

Pour the mussel pan liquid through a fine sieve, to remove any grit, directly into the vegetable pan. Add the turmeric or saffron, cayenne and black pepper to taste. Simmer very gently, covered.

Remove the mussels from their shells (some people might prefer to leave them on the half shell). They should be added all at once, with the wine, to the oniony stock. Replace the lid and leave to simmer very gently for a further 3-5 minutes.

Add the cream (if using) and parsley, and serve in shallow soup plates with lots of hot bread.

Baked Eggs

My entire household has rediscovered baked eggs, with the result that the sink is now full of little ramekins instead of pans coated with burned scrambled egg. Baked eggs take longer to cook but taste subtly nicer, either quite plain, or fancied up with herbs, chopped mushroom, bacon, etc. The method may sound fussy for such a simple dish, but practise it until it becomes effortless because it makes for eggs which are sufficiently set to turn out, but still creamy and delicious.

1 SERVING

a scrap of butter and/or 1 teaspoon   *1-2 eggs*
   soured cream
salt and pepper
optional extras: ½ teaspoon chopped
   fresh herbs, or 1 teaspoon chopped
   mushroom or bacon

Put all the ingredients, except the egg, in a ramekin dish. Stand it in a shallow ovenproof dish with hot water in it to come about 1 cm (½ inch) up the sides. Pop this dish in the oven at 190°C (375°F) mark 5 for a few minutes or until the butter is hot and the mushroom, or whatever you are using, is starting to cook. Wearing oven gloves, take the dish out and break the egg into the ramekin. Return to the oven with a lid or piece of foil on top. I find this speeds the cooking. Cook for 10-12 minutes or until the white is opaque and the yolk just setting.

Baked eggs can be eaten with teaspoons straight from the dish, or turned out on to plates to eat with fried bacon, or a salad, or buttered toast.

Spinach Salad with Frizzled Bacon and Croûtons

This is an up-date on the old rustic French salad of young dandelion leaves wilted in the fat rendered from diced bacon and served with a dash of vinegar.

If you can lay hands on some new dandelion leaves (the smaller inner ones), they add a certain *je ne sais quoi* to the spinach, which must be young, green and crisped in cold water beforehand.

4 SERVINGS

450 g (1 lb) spinach leaves
1 small slice of fatty gammon (see page 13), cubed, or 4 rashers of streaky bacon, de-rinded and cut into strips
1-2 tablespoons white or red wine vinegar

FOR THE CROÛTONS
1 thick slice of day-old bread
1 garlic clove, halved
1 tablespoon olive oil
a knob of butter

Pick over the spinach, discarding any limp or yellowing leaves and pinching off coarse stalks. Leave in cold water for 1-2 hours to crisp.

To make the croûtons, cut the crusts off the bread and rub it with the garlic clove, then dice the bread into cubes. Heat the oil and butter in a frying pan and fry the bread cubes until golden. Remove from the pan and keep warm.

Put the gammon or bacon in the pan and heat gently until the fat runs and the meat is cooked.

Drain the spinach and dry it in a salad spinner or shake it in a clean towel, then put it in a bowl, and quickly add the gammon or bacon and the croûtons. Pour the vinegar into the pan, swirl round and pour over the spinach. Toss well and serve on cold plates.

Mashed Potato and Swede

It seems incredible that there was a time when I despised swedes, now a household favourite, especially cooked like this. I know the snobbery persists in France, however. I produced this dish for a Frenchman once; he pronounced it intriguing and good, and asked what went into it. On hearing it was swedes, he looked scandalised. But that is cattle food! Choose smallish swedes, which are likely to be younger, and tender once cooked. Every now and then one encounters a swede that retains a woody core even after the longest cooking; best chuck these, they have been around too long. A prime swede yields sweet, golden flesh of a delicious texture, less perfumed than parsnip, tastier than pumpkin. It can also be made into a flavoursome soup.

4 SERVINGS

1 swede, weighing about 450-700 g
  (1-1½ lb), scrubbed
700 g (1½ lb) 'floury' potatoes, such
  as King Edward or Maris Piper,
  scrubbed

50 g (2 oz) butter
250 ml (8 fl oz) milk
salt and pepper
freshly grated nutmeg

Put the swede in a large saucepan, cover with cold water and bring slowly to the boil, then reduce the heat and simmer for 45 minutes-1 hour or until tender. Meanwhile, put the potatoes in another large saucepan and cover with cold water. Bring to the boil, then reduce the heat and simmer for 20–25 minutes or until tender. Drain the potatoes and peel them, wearing rubber gloves. Cut the potatoes roughly into chunks and put them in a heatproof bowl. Mash the potatoes with a potato masher until soft, then beat in the butter and milk to give a smooth, soft consistency. Cover and keep warm.

When the swede is tender enough to yield to a fork, drain, peel, cut into chunks and mash in the same way as the potato. Mix the swede with the mashed potato, beating with a fork to amalgamate thoroughly. Season well with salt, pepper and nutmeg, adding more butter and milk if the mixture seems too stiff. Serve hot.

French Fried Onion Rings

 There is a trick to making these crisp, puffy, golden fried onion rings, which is worth learning. Some people will eat almost anything provided you dish up a pile of these onions at the same time.

4 SERVINGS

4 onions, very thinly sliced into rings
salt

50 g (2 oz) plain flour
vegetable oil for deep frying

Sprinkle the onions with salt and leave on a plate for 20 minutes or so, to sweat out their moisture.

Drain the onions, shake off excess salt and dredge with flour (the easiest way to do this is to put the flour in a paper bag and to shake the onions around inside it). Fry the onions in hot oil for 5 minutes.

Take the onions out of the pan with a perforated slice. Reheat the oil until it is good and hot, then return the onions to the pan and fry until as crisp and golden as you want them. Drain on kitchen paper.

NOTE: *This is also the French method of producing those delicious* frites *(chips) which taste so different from the sluggish white things most British chippies produce. The trick is to fry twice, with a pause in between for the oil to heat up again.*

Roast Onions

Not only are onions almost the cheapest vegetable, but if you believe time is money, this is a terrific recipe for paupers.

4 SERVINGS
4 even-sized onions

Stand the onions in an ovenproof dish and roast them in their skins in the oven at 180°C (350°F) mark 4 for about 1 hour. They give off a delicious smell of caramel.

Braised Cabbage with Apple

After washing the cabbage, don't be fussy about drying it; the water that adheres to the leaves will provide its cooking liquid.

6 SERVINGS
50 g (2 oz) butter
1 small onion, sliced
1 green or red cabbage, chopped
2 Cox's Orange Pippin, or other
  firm eating apples, peeled, cored
  and sliced

2 teaspoons soft brown sugar
a pinch of salt

Melt the butter in a saucepan, add the onion, cover with a lid and cook over a very low heat, stirring occasionally, until the onion is soft but not brown. Add the cabbage, apple, sugar and salt. Stir, then replace the lid and cook over a very gentle heat for 20–30 minutes, stirring once or twice, until the cabbage is tender but still fresh-tasting.

NOTE: *If you want to make the cabbage more tart, add 1 tablespoon cider vinegar with the raw cabbage and other ingredients.*

Braised Celery

6-8 SERVINGS

4 heads of celery   *450 ml (¾ pint) hot vegetable stock*

Trim the celery heads, remove the tough outside stalks and scrape off any strings with a sharp knife. Cut each head in half lengthways.

Simmer the celery pieces in salted water for 10 minutes, then drain and put them in an earthenware or other gratin dish which is broad enough to hold them side by side. Cover with hot stock, cover and cook in the oven at 140°C (275°F) mark 1 for 1 hour or until the stock has reduced to a syrup.

'Hot' Cauliflower

4-6 SERVINGS

4 garlic cloves   *4 tablespoons dried breadcrumbs*
3 anchovy fillets   *1 dried red chilli, finely chopped*
1 cauliflower, broken into florets   *2 tablespoons finely chopped fresh*
2 tablespoons olive oil   * parsley*
25 g (1 oz) butter

Crush the garlic in a pestle and mortar or in a strong bowl with the end of a rolling pin. Add the anchovy fillets and pound to a paste. Steam or briefly cook the cauliflower florets in boiling salted water for about 5 minutes or until just tender but still slightly crisp.

Meanwhile, heat the oil and butter in a frying pan and fry the breadcrumbs and chilli until golden. Add the mixture from the mortar and stir in the chopped parsley.

Drain the cauliflower, if necessary, and place in a warmed serving bowl. Spoon over the breadcrumb mixture.

Broad Beans in a Pot with Bacon

For broad beans late in the season, when they are large and have tough husks.

5-6 SERVINGS AS PART OF A MEAL

450 g (1 lb) shelled broad beans   *salt and pepper*
3 rashers of back bacon, de-rinded   *a bunch of fresh mint or coriander,*
2 tablespoons olive oil   * chopped*
1 small onion, sliced

To skin the beans, make a lengthways cut in the skin of each one and squeeze the bean gently until it slips out of its skin. Cut the bacon into matchsticks and put it in a flameproof casserole or earthenware pot. Heat gently to sweat the moisture out of the bacon and to melt its fat. Add the oil and continue cooking until the bacon is just cooked but not yet beginning to brown. Add the onion and cook until golden, then add the beans, season with salt and pepper, cover with a lid and continue cooking for a few more minutes until the beans are tender, adding a splash of water if the mixture looks as if it is drying out. Add the herbs 30 seconds before you remove the dish from the heat.

Potatoes with Rosemary, Bacon and Cream

This is a very good way to cook potatoes to go with plainly baked fish or chicken breasts. There is no need to peel the potatoes as long as they are smooth and thin-skinned.

4 SERVINGS

700 g (1½ lb) potatoes, scrubbed and thinly sliced

4 rashers of streaky bacon, de-rinded and cut into thin strips

4 garlic cloves, thinly sliced

about 2 sprigs of fresh rosemary, or 1 tablespoon dried

300 ml (½ pint) single cream

about 50 g (2 oz) butter

Layer the slices of potato in a buttered or oiled baking dish or tin, scattering the bacon, garlic and fragments of rosemary between the layers. Pour the cream over and dot with the butter. Lay a piece of foil or greaseproof paper over the top and cook in the oven at 200°C (400°F) mark 6 for 20 minutes. Remove the foil and cook for a further 20 minutes or until the top is golden brown and the potatoes tender.

N O T E : *Depending on the type of potatoes you use, you may need to leave the covering in place for more or less time so that the potatoes cook before they dry out.*

Kedgeree

6 SERVINGS

450 g (1 lb) smoked haddock
50 g (2 oz) butter
2 onions, sliced
1 teaspoon curry powder
salt and black pepper
450 g (1 lb) 'easy-cook' long-grain
rice

3 hard-boiled eggs, sliced
a large sprig of fresh parsley, finely
chopped
125 ml (4 fl oz) single or whipping
cream

Put the haddock in a saucepan, cover with water and simmer gently for 15–20 minutes or until the fish comes off the skin easily. Take the fish out of its simmering liquid and carefully flake the fish, removing all the skin and bones.

Melt the butter in a heavy-based saucepan and fry the onions until they have turned golden. Add the curry powder and cook for 1 minute, then remove from the heat.

Put the haddock cooking liquid in a saucepan, top it up with more water, and bring to the boil. Add salt to taste, stir in the rice and simmer for about 10 minutes or until it is just tender. Drain it well and stir it into the curried buttery onions. Gently fold in the flaked haddock and the sliced hard-boiled eggs. Season liberally with pepper and finally stir in the chopped parsley and the cream. Serve immediately.

Fish Pie

There are dozens of more or less elaborate versions of fish pie. To my mind, the simple, classic version given here, combining fish and hard-boiled egg in a creamy and faintly cheesy white sauce, is the best of all. The preparation and cooking should be done with care.

Any firm white fish can be used: cod, bream, bass. Coley, if you can get it, is an excellent cheap substitute for cod, with a dark meat which turns white when cooked, and a good flavour. For economy's sake you can omit the shrimps.

34

2 SERVINGS

225 g (8 oz) white fish
1 bay leaf (optional)
40 g (1½ oz) butter
25 g (1 oz) plain flour
milk
salt and pepper

50 g (2 oz) Cheddar cheese, grated
½ teaspoon mustard powder
50 g (2 oz) peeled shrimps
  (optional)
2 hard-boiled eggs, chopped
dried breadcrumbs or mashed potato

Put the fish in a baking dish with a little water. Add the bay leaf, if using, cover and bake in the oven at 180°C (350°F) mark 4 for 20-30 minutes. Drain the fish on to a plate, reserving the cooking water. Divide the fish into chunks, removing any skin and bones.

Melt 25 g (1 oz) of the butter in a saucepan and stir in the flour. Cook for 1-2 minutes, stirring, then remove from the heat. Make up the reserved fish stock to 300 ml (½ pint) with milk and stir gradually into the butter and flour mixture. Bring to the boil, stirring constantly, then simmer for a few minutes until smooth and thick. Season with salt and pepper and stir in the cheese and mustard. Remove from the heat and stir in the fish, shrimps, if using, and hard-boiled egg. Turn into an ovenproof dish. Either sprinkle the top with breadcrumbs, or spread a layer of mashed potatoes over it, dot with the remaining butter and bake in the oven at 180°C (350°F) mark 4 until the top is brown.

Baked Tomatoes (see page 119) go nicely with this.

 ## Soft Herring Roes with Peas

This is an excellent supper dish with baked or boiled potatoes; it is also good as a starter on toast or even for a sumptuous breakfast.

4 SERVINGS

225 g (8 oz) shelled fresh or frozen
  peas
50 g (2 oz) butter

2 garlic cloves, crushed
450 g (1 lb) soft herring roes
salt and black pepper

Blanch the frozen peas in boiling salted water, or if you are using fresh peas boil them until they are barely cooked. 'Refresh' them under gently flowing cold water, drain and set aside.

Melt the butter with the garlic in a heavy-based frying pan until it is hot but not burned. Add the herring roes, a few at a time. (There is no need to remove the first roes from the pan, just add them gradually so that the butter stays hot and seals each roe. There is no hope of the roes all staying crisp and separate as many will be a bit smashed before they reach you, but it helps the flavour to have some which are brown on the edges.) When they are all hot and bubbling, add the peas, heat through, season lavishly with black pepper and sparingly with salt, and serve very hot.

VARIATION: The identical recipe can be made with chicken livers, but with the addition of some bits of crispy bacon.

Braised Herrings with Potatoes and Apple

5 SERVINGS

450 g (1 lb) herring fillets
75 g (3 oz) butter, softened
2 tablespoons prepared mustard
    (optional)
salt and black pepper
900 g (2 lb) potatoes, peeled and
    thinly sliced

2 large, firm apples, peeled, cored
    and thinly sliced
2 onions, thinly sliced
300 ml (½ pint) cider or water

Lay the herring fillets skin-side down and spread them with 65 g (2½ oz) of the butter and the mustard, if using. Season with black pepper and a little salt and roll them up, skin-side out.

Butter a fairly deep ovenproof dish (earthenware would be ideal) and put in half the potato slices, then one of the sliced apples and one of the onions. Lay the herring rolls on top, and cover them with the rest of the onion and apple, and finally the remaining potato slices. Pour over the cider or water to come halfway up the side of the dish. Dot the top with the remaining butter and grind a little salt and pepper over it. Cover with foil and bake in the oven at 180°C (350°F) mark 4 for 30 minutes, then remove the foil and turn the oven up to 200°C (400°F) mark 6 and cook for a further 30 minutes or until the top is golden. If it threatens to dry out before the potatoes are cooked, you can add a little more liquid.

Mussel and Potato Hotpot

Mussels are still the best value in seafood, and a rare example of how farming can improve the product; I find farmed mussels need less cleaning, their flavour is unimpaired, and they are available all year round. This recipe makes a substantial and tasty meal, with a layer of mussels and bacon sandwiched between sliced potatoes and onions. The dish comes from Darina Allen, of Ballymaloe Cookery School fame, but I have adapted the original recipe a little to meet pauper requirements.

4-6 SERVINGS

4 tablespoons olive, sunflower or safflower oil

2 large onions, chopped

3 rashers of streaky bacon, de-rinded and diced

1 kg (2¼ lb) fresh mussels

300 ml (½ pint) dry white wine or dry cider

a large handful of fresh parsley, chopped

2 sprigs of fresh thyme, chopped

150 ml (5 fl oz) carton of single cream

salt and pepper

about 450 g (1 lb) cooked potatoes, peeled and sliced

25 g (1 oz) butter

3-4 tablespoons dried or fresh breadcrumbs

2-3 tablespoons grated cheese, eg a good Cheddar or Parmesan

2 garlic cloves, chopped

Heat the oil in a heavy-based saucepan, add the onion and bacon, cover and sweat over a low heat until the onion is soft and transparent.

Meanwhile, pick over the mussels, checking that they are all tightly closed. Scrub them well and pull off any beards with a knife. Put the wine or cider in a stainless steel or enamel pan, add half the parsley and the thyme and heat until bubbling. Tip in the mussels, clap the lid on the pan and cook over a moderate heat for about 3 minutes, then check to see if they have opened. As soon as all the mussels have opened, spoon them on to a plate and leave to cool. (Discard any mussels that do not open.) Strain the cooking liquor, add the cream and season with salt and pepper.

Layer half the sliced potatoes with half the onion and bacon mixture in a gratin dish. Take the mussels from their shells (I use a small knife; they can be quite tricky to remove whole) and spread them over the vegetables, then finish up with more layers of onion and potato. Pour over the creamy liquor.

Melt the butter in a saucepan, add the breadcrumbs and turn them in the butter over a low heat for a moment, until golden, then mix them with the remaining parsley, the grated cheese and the chopped garlic. Spread this mixture over the top of the dish and bake in the oven at 180°C (350°F) mark 4 until the top is crisp and the contents bubbling hot. Serve with steamed broccoli or a crunchy green salad made with frisée, chicory or a mixture.

Stuffed Cabbage

There are dozens of recipes for this dish, which is a well-established favourite in almost every country in Europe – except England, where cabbage is not usually given such respectful treatment. The version I use, given here, is quicker to prepare than most, not very elegant perhaps, but it tastes just as good. Choose a cabbage with thick, sturdy leaves. If you like, you can cut down on the amount of tomato sauce or stock used and add cider instead.

4-6 SERVINGS

1 large green cabbage
a knob of butter
2 onions, chopped
225 g (8 oz) minced beef or good
   sausagemeat
a sprig of fresh thyme, chopped, or
   1 teaspoon dried

2 garlic cloves, chopped
a dash of soy sauce
1-2 tablespoons chopped fresh parsley
450-600 ml (¾-1 pint) Tomato
   Sauce (see page 45) or Simple
   Stock (see page 21)

Trim the stalk and the ragged outer leaves off the cabbage. Plunge the whole cabbage into boiling water and cook, covered, for 5-6 minutes. Drain.

Prepare the stuffing by melting the butter in a frying pan and gently frying the onions until they begin to soften. Add the meat, thyme and garlic. When this has browned a little, add the soy sauce. Turn off the heat and stir in the parsley.

Peel back two layers of leaves from around the cabbage, taking care not to break them. With a sharp, pointed knife, cut the centre of the cabbage out, leaving a wall all round and doing your best not to cut through the outer case. This is not all that easy to do – perhaps the best way is to start by removing a small core and hollowing the rest out with a spoon. Pack the stuffing into the cavity and cover with a piece of the cabbage you cut out. Fold the outer leaves back into place and tie with string. Place the cabbage in a deep, round casserole, pour on the tomato sauce or stock, packing in any remaining odd bits of cabbage, chopped coarsely, cover and bake in the oven at 200°C (400°F) mark 6 for 1 hour. Spoon a little of the liquid over it from time to time.

All you need with this is boiled rice.

Baked Stuffed Vegetable Marrow

Large vegetable marrows are very cheap in season and make a handy receptacle for a highly seasoned minced meat stuffing, the bland flavour of the marrow providing just enough contrast. It is a less solid and indigestible dish than stuffed green peppers or aubergines, and I think rather nicer. Add a few raisins, sultanas or currants to the stuffing, if liked.

4-6 SERVINGS

1 medium-sized marrow (about
   30.5 cm/12 inches long)
a knob of butter
2-3 rashers of bacon, de-rinded and
   cut into small squares
2 onions, chopped
2-4 garlic cloves, chopped
225 g (8 oz) minced beef or lamb

400 g (14 oz) can of tomatoes
a sprig of fresh thyme, marjoram or
   fennel, chopped, or 1 teaspoon
   dried
salt and pepper
25 g (1 oz) long-grain rice, cooked
   (see page 58)
a little sugar

Bring a large saucepan of water to the boil, plunge in the marrow and cook for 3 minutes. Remove. Slice off the top of the marrow, lengthways, about one third from the top so you have one deeper marrow receptacle and one shallow lid. Scoop out the seeds and membrane, and a little pulp if the space looks too shallow.

Melt the butter in a frying pan and fry the bacon, the onions and garlic. Add the minced meat and fry gently until lightly browned. Drain the can of tomatoes and add a little of the juice to the meat mixture to moisten it. Add the herbs and season well with salt and pepper. Stir in the cooked rice. If the mixture seems very dry, add more tomato liquid. Fill the scooped-out marrow with the mixture, put on the lid and secure with string or a couple of skewers. Put the canned tomatoes in a saucepan with a little salt, sugar and pepper and cook gently until they can be mashed to a pulp. Dilute with water if too thick. Put the marrow in a roasting tin or baking dish and pour the tomato pulp around it. Bake in the oven at 180°C (350°F) mark 4 for 1 hour or until the marrow is tender, basting from time to time with the tomato sauce.

Serve with plain boiled rice, and the juice from the pan.

Shepherd's Pie

Revising this book, I was amazed to find no recipe for shepherd's pie, made with minced lamb or mutton, or cottage pie, made with beef. Perhaps I thought it was too familiar to be worth including. Anyway, I'm grateful for the chance to repair the omission because this is the friendliest of our native dishes. Originally, shepherd's pie was a made-up dish, an ideal way to stretch leftover cooked meat. Today, I tend to make it with fresh minced lamb from a hallal butcher, for preference, because (a) their lamb verges on mutton, and so is tastier, and (b) because the quality is consistently high, due to rapid turnover.

6-8 SERVINGS

700 g (1½ lb) 'floury' potatoes	2 medium-sized onions, chopped
salt and black pepper	Worcestershire or soy sauce
700 g (1½ lb) fresh minced lamb or mutton	tomato purée (optional)
	25 g (1 oz) butter
225 g (8 oz) carrots, sliced	25 ml (1 fl oz) milk

Put the unpeeled potatoes in a large saucepan of salted water and bring to the boil. Reduce the heat and leave to simmer while preparing the pie filling.

Put the minced meat in a heavy-based saucepan, cover and set over a gentle heat to render off some fat. It will need an occasional stir, with a wooden fork if possible, to ensure the meat heats through thoroughly and to break up lumps.

Meanwhile, bring a saucepan of salted water to the boil and add the carrots. Bring back to the boil and, after 3 minutes, add the onions and cook for 1-2 minutes longer. (This is a softening procedure, *not* meant to cook the vegetables through.) Drain the vegetables, reserving the liquid. Chop the carrots even smaller.

By now, the meat should have yielded quite a bit of fat. Pour this off – I tend to chuck it, though in the old days people swore by mutton fat for chapped hands or cracked leather! Mix the minced meat with the carrots and onions, season generously with salt and black pepper and moisten with a little of the reserved vegetable water plus a good splash of Worcester or soy sauce, or both. I sometimes add a squeeze of tomato purée, more for colour than anything else. Spread this mixture in a shallow oval or round ovenproof dish, with sloping sides, if possible – the classic British shape.

40

The potatoes should now feel soft when prodded with a fork, but not so soft that they disintegrate. Drain the potatoes, peel when cool enough to handle, and mash while still hot, adding half the butter and the milk, and salt and pepper to taste. The mash should be more solid than the usual purée, to make a decent topping for the pie. Spoon the potato over the meat mixture, smoothing it out with a fork, then roughing up the surface to help it brown. Dot with the remaining butter and cook in the oven at 190°C (375°F) mark 5 for 30–40 minutes or until the top is lightly browned.

Serve with buttered greens, cabbage or sprouts, and more carrots. Hand round Worcester sauce and ketchup, too.

Rillons

Much modern pork is improved by steeping it in salt for a few hours; wash it off and dry the meat before cooking.

6-8 SERVINGS

900 g (2 lb) belly of pork
a sprig of fresh thyme

1 bay leaf
salt and black pepper

Cut the belly of pork into 5 cm (2 inch) cubes and put them in a heavy-based saucepan or flameproof casserole with 175–250 ml (6–8 fl oz) water, the thyme and bay leaf. Cover and cook over a gentle heat or in the oven at 140°C (275°F) mark 1 for 4 hours.

Drain off the fat and reserve to use for cooking on another occasion. Put the *rillons* back in the pan and continue to cook, uncovered, over a higher heat or in the oven at 190°C (375°F) mark 5 until brown. Season with salt and pepper and eat with mashed potatoes and baked apples.

Pork and Beans

This recipe is a classic of American domestic cookery and the inspiration, I imagine, of the ubiquitous baked beans. It is easy to make.

4-6 SERVINGS

450 g (1 lb) dried haricot beans,
*   soaked overnight*
2 tablespoons black treacle (molasses)
a dash of Worcestershire sauce
2 teaspoons mustard powder
2 teaspoons brown sugar

salt and pepper
225 g (8 oz) belly of pork or streaky
*   bacon, de-rinded and roughly*
*   chopped*
1 large onion, sliced

41

Drain the haricot beans, reserving the soaking water. Heat the bean water and stir into it the treacle, Worcestershire sauce, mustard, sugar, salt and pepper. Mix up the beans, pork and onion in a casserole, pour over the bean water and add more hot water if necessary to come just over the top of the beans. Cover and bake in the oven at 180°C (350°F) mark 4 for 2½-3 hours, or until the beans are soft. Look at it once or twice during this time, and, if the beans seem to be getting too dry, add more hot water.

Onion, Bacon and Potato Hotpot

If I were restricted to cooking the same three recipes for the rest of my life, this would definitely be on the list. I got it from my mother, who can't remember where she got it from, and friends and acquaintances have been copying it ever since. It is very cheap, makes use of ingredients generally to hand, and tastes – I think – particularly delicious.

The bacon need not be rashers – scraps of cooked bacon leftover from a boiled joint will do just as well. You can use more or less bacon, as convenient. About 2 tablespoons grated cheese can be added to the white sauce.

4 SERVINGS

50 g (2 oz) butter
50 g (2 oz) plain flour
568 ml (1 pint) milk
salt and pepper
freshly grated nutmeg (optional)

4 large onions, very thinly sliced
4 large potatoes, peeled and very thinly sliced
125-225 g (4-8 oz) bacon rashers, de-rinded and cut into small strips

Melt the butter in a saucepan and stir in the flour. Remove from the heat and gradually stir in the milk. Bring to the boil, stirring constantly until smooth and thick, then reduce the heat. Add salt and pepper, and nutmeg if you like, and leave the sauce simmering gently on an asbestos mat while you prepare the rest of the dish.

Grease a casserole and fill it with alternate layers of sliced onions, sliced potatoes and bacon strips, ending with a layer of potato. Pour over the white sauce. Give the casserole a good shake to distribute the sauce throughout. Cover, and bake in the oven at 200°C (400°F) mark 6 for 1 hour, then reduce the heat to 180°C (350°F) mark 4, uncover the casserole and cook for a further 1 hour.

This is really a winter dish, and goes best with winter vegetables like Brussels sprouts and cabbage.

Keema Matar

This is authentic Indian home cooking; useful for the pauper who only has a couple of rings and a couple of pans. You will need a pan which will fry food and also has a lid – a sauté pan or a fairly wide-bottomed saucepan with a lid, or a cast-iron casserole.

6-8 SERVINGS

2 teaspoons coriander seeds
2 teaspoons cumin seeds
3 tablespoons vegetable oil
2 onions, finely chopped
6 garlic cloves, crushed
2.5 cm (1 inch) piece of fresh root
    ginger, peeled and finely chopped
1 fresh or dried chilli, de-seeded and
    finely chopped

700 g (1½ lb) minced lamb
75 ml (3 fl oz) water
450 g (1 lb) shelled fresh or frozen
    peas
salt
1 teaspoon garam masala
a large sprig of fresh mint or
    coriander, finely chopped

Pound the coriander and cumin seeds in a mortar, or in a strong bowl with the end of a rolling pin, or grind them in a (cleaned) coffee grinder. Heat the oil in a wide-bottomed pan and fry the onions until golden. Add the garlic and fry for 1 minute, then add the crushed seeds, ginger and chilli, stir for a minute and add the mince. Brown the mince, stirring it round for 5 minutes, then pour over the water. Bring to the boil, then reduce the heat, cover and simmer for 20 minutes.

Add the peas – if they are frozen they will cook very quickly but fresh peas may need a little more water added with them. Taste the mince and add salt at this stage. Stir in the garam masala, replace the lid and continue to cook for a few minutes. Add the mint or coriander about 2 minutes before serving with basmati or long-grain rice.

Spiced Beef Loaf

6-8 SERVINGS

3 garlic cloves
1 teaspoon juniper berries
1 tablespoon peppercorns
1 teaspoon allspice (berries or
    ground)

1 heaped teaspoon salt
5 rashers of streaky bacon, de-rinded
    and finely chopped
900 g (2 lb) minced beef
1 glass of red wine

Chop the garlic very finely and lightly crush it in a mortar with the juniper berries, peppercorns, allspice and salt. Mix the bacon and spices into the minced beef with the wine, and leave for a few hours in a cold place.

Pack the meat mixture tightly into a loaf tin and stand it in a baking tin full of water. Cook in the oven at 170°C (325°F) mark 3 for 1½ hours, only covering it with foil if it seems to be burning on the top. Leave to cool and, when it is quite cold, turn the loaf out with the help of a knife. Cut thinly and eat with baked potatoes, pickles and salad.

Gingered Pork Balls with Peas

6 SERVINGS

4 garlic cloves	2 tablespoons plain flour
450 g (1 lb) minced pork	sunflower oil
5 cm (2 inch) piece of fresh root ginger, peeled and finely chopped	225 g (8 oz) mushrooms
	2 tablespoons sesame oil
a bunch of fresh coriander, finely chopped	450 g (1 lb) frozen peas, thawed
	3-4 tablespoons dry sherry
salt and pepper	2 tablespoons soy sauce
1 egg	

Finely chop two of the garlic cloves and stir them into the minced pork with the ginger and coriander. Season with salt and pepper and stir in the egg. Make the pork into small balls about 2.5 cm (1 inch) in diameter, rolling them lightly in flour seasoned with salt and pepper. Heat a little sunflower oil in a heavy-based frying pan (use the minimum you need to prevent the balls from sticking) and fry the pork balls until golden. Remove the balls to a warm dish.

Chop the mushrooms fairly coarsely so that the pieces will retain some bite, and finely chop the remaining garlic cloves. When all the balls are done, pour away any oil that is still in the pan, leaving just a tablespoonful. Add about 1 tablespoon sesame oil, the garlic and the mushrooms and fry over a moderate heat until cooked. Pour over the balls. Add the remaining tablespoon of sesame oil to the pan and pour in the peas. When these are hot, pour them over the balls and mushrooms. Pour the sherry into the pan, cook for a few seconds until reduced slightly and then pour over the pork balls. Season with soy sauce and serve with rice or noodles.

Meat Balls in Tomato Sauce

6 SERVINGS

FOR THE MEAT BALLS
1 large onion, finely chopped
6 garlic cloves, finely chopped
a bunch of fresh parsley or coriander,
    finely chopped
450 g (1 lb) minced lamb or beef
salt and black pepper
2 teaspoons ground cumin (if using
    lamb)
1 egg
sunflower oil for frying

FOR THE TOMATO SAUCE
2 × 400 g (14 oz) can of tomatoes
2-6 garlic cloves
2 tablespoons olive oil
a splash of wine (optional)
1 teaspoon sugar
1 sprig of fresh thyme or basil,
    chopped
salt and pepper

To make the sauce, simmer all the ingredients together in a heavy-based saucepan or flameproof casserole for about 1 hour or until the garlic melts. Season with salt and pepper.

Mix the onion, garlic and herbs into the minced meat (best done with your hands), seasoning the mixture with salt and pepper, and cumin if you are using lamb. Lastly, mix in the egg. Flour your hands and start to form the mixture into small golf balls, leaving them on a floured surface.

Heat plenty of sunflower oil (about 0.5 cm/¼ inch deep) in a large, heavy-based frying pan and begin to fry the balls in batches until they are browned all over. As you remove them from the pan they can be placed in a casserole. When they are all in the casserole, pour over the tomato sauce. The dish can be kept warm in the oven for up to 1 hour until you need it – the balls will not disintegrate – or left to cool and re-heated later. Serve with plenty of pasta, rice or potatoes.

 ## Slow-Cooked Chickpeas and Kidneys

This dish is quite different from the more usual bean and pork combinations. It is rich and warming and very inexpensive. Beef kidney makes a good gravy which marries curiously with the nuttiness of the chickpeas. To make a meatier dish, gently melt the 'suet' from around the kidney to fry the onions in instead of the olive oil. However, only a real butcher will sell you this – you never see fresh suet in the supermarket.

8 SERVINGS

450 g (1 lb) dried chickpeas, soaked
    overnight
5 tablespoons olive oil or melted beef
    suet
2 onions, finely sliced
3 garlic cloves, finely sliced
450 g (1 lb) beef kidney, cored and
    roughly chopped

salt and black pepper
a sprig of fresh thyme
2 bay leaves
a sprig of fresh parsley
900 ml (1½ pints) water
1 teaspoon whole grain mustard

Drain the chickpeas and put them in a large saucepan. Cover with fresh water, bring to the boil and boil quite hard for about 40 minutes, then drain.

Meanwhile, heat the oil or melted suet in a flameproof casserole or frying pan and fry the onions and garlic until soft. Add the kidney and cook until just sealed. Remove from the heat. If you are using a casserole, remove the kidney mixture and put half the chickpeas in the bottom of the casserole. Season with salt and pepper, cover with the kidney, season again – I think it's hard to overdo the pepper – and put the rest of the chickpeas on top. Tie the herbs together with string to make a bouquet garni and bury it in the chickpeas, then pour over the water. Put the lid on and cook in the oven at 150°C (300°F) mark 2 for 5–6 hours. Alternatively, cook at 170°C (325°F) mark 3 for 3 hours. It is important that the lid should be tight fitting: if you suspect it, you may either seal it stylishly with a flour and water paste, or easier (and probably safer until you have tried this recipe in your oven, with your particular pans, etc.), use an extra seal of kitchen foil under the lid. A few minutes before serving, remove the bouquet garni and stir in the mustard.

This dish needs only something green to go with it, raw or plainly cooked.

 ## Liver in the Venetian Manner

Fried liver and onions is a well-known combination. The Venetian way of preparing it is the nicest of all, the onions stewed slowly and gently in a little oil, with the liver – cut into small, thin strips – stirred in towards the end.

2 SERVINGS

vegetable oil for frying

225 g (8 oz) onions, very finely
   sliced

salt and pepper

125 g (4 oz) calves' or lamb's liver

Cover the bottom of a heavy-based frying pan (if your pan is light-weight, keep an asbestos mat underneath it) with a thin layer of oil. Add the onions, season with salt and pepper, cover and cook gently for 30–40 minutes.

Meanwhile, with a very sharp knife, shave thinnest possible slices off the liver. If it is calves' liver, it will only need 2-3 minutes' cooking with the onions, but if it is lamb's liver you will need to add it to the onions after about 30 minutes and cook for another 15 minutes.

You can serve this just as it is, or with plain boiled rice. It is a particularly warming dish in winter.

Sweet and Sour Liver and Onions

 Unglamorous ingredients, stylishly turned out. Pig's liver is the cheapest type of liver, if you like its rather strong flavour.

4-6 SERVINGS

2 onions, finely sliced

sunflower oil for frying

700 g (1½ lb) liver

salt and pepper

3 garlic cloves, chopped

1 tablespoon brown sugar

3 tablespoons vinegar (wine, sherry
   or balsamic)

1 sprig of fresh coriander or mint,
   chopped (optional)

Fry the onions quickly in oil until just turning colour. Remove and keep hot. Slice the liver very finely, trimming it of any veinous bits, and season with salt and pepper. Fry it very quickly in the pan the onions were in, adding another tablespoon or so of oil if necessary, until crisp on the outside. Remove to the warm dish.

Heat the garlic in the oil, adding the sugar after a second (ie before the garlic begins to cook). Heat them together gently until the sugar is melted and golden. Pour in the vinegar and let it sizzle for a minute, then pour the sauce over the liver. Season liberally with pepper and, if you have it, sprinkle with a little chopped fresh coriander or mint.

Oxtail Stew

Oxtail makes a rich, thick stew with a good meaty flavour. The pieces of tail should be washed, dipped in boiling water and dried before frying with the onions.

4-6 SERVINGS

1 medium-sized oxtail, jointed
1 tablespoon plain flour
salt and pepper
25 g (1 oz) butter
2 onions, sliced
2 carrots, sliced

1 celery stick, sliced
1 turnip, sliced
2 cloves
a pinch of ground mace
juice of ½ lemon

Separate the jointed pieces of oxtail, if necessary. Wash them, dip them in boiling water for 1 minute, then dry them carefully. Roll the pieces in the flour, seasoned with salt and pepper.

Melt the butter in a large, heavy-based saucepan or flameproof casserole and put in the pieces of meat and sliced onions when it is sizzling. Turn them over so that the meat browns on all sides. Add the remaining vegetables, the cloves, mace and enough water to cover the lot. Bring to the boil, skimming off any froth which rises to the top. Reduce the heat to simmering, and cover the pan with a piece of kitchen foil or greaseproof paper and the lid. Simmer very slowly for 3 hours, or longer if you are not in a hurry, or until the meat is falling off the bone.

Taste the stock and add salt and pepper, if needed. Should you feel up to it, the appearance of the dish will be improved if you pick out the pieces of meat and put the stock and vegetables through a sieve, returning the thickened stock and meat to the pan for a few minutes to heat up again. Either way, add the lemon juice just before serving.

Plainly cooked, homely vegetables go best with oxtail – boiled potatoes, carrots, cabbage.

Spare Ribs

Little jars of sun-dried tomatoes in olive oil are exorbitantly expensive. Buy them dry when you can from a delicatessen or Italian shop and preserve them in oil and herbs yourself.

The quantities given in this recipe are enough for six if you will all be contented with one rib each. Serve a hearty rice dish to go with it.

6 SERVINGS

6 meaty spare ribs
1 tablespoon soy sauce
6 garlic cloves, finely chopped
vegetable oil
2 green peppers, de-seeded and cut
  into chunks

1 tablespoon chopped sun-dried
  tomatoes
1 sprig of fresh coriander, chopped
black pepper

When you bring the pork home, or at least 30 minutes before cooking, put the spare ribs into the earthenware pot or casserole in which you are going to cook them and sprinkle them with the soy sauce and three of the finely chopped garlic cloves.

Cook the spare ribs, uncovered, in the oven at 180°C (350°F) mark 4. They do not need any extra fat or moisture as they produce their own. When they seem just cooked but not brown, heat a little oil in a heavy-based frying pan and sear the peppers and remaining garlic. Remove the peppers to the ribs pot and put the ribs (without their juice) in the frying pan. Pour the hot pork juices into a bowl. Cook the ribs until brown, then sprinkle the tomato pieces over them. Stir it around a bit, then put the ribs back in the pot with the peppers. Pour the juices which came from their first cooking into the frying pan and let them sizzle. Pour back over the meat and peppers, sprinkle on the coriander, season with black pepper and return to the oven for a further 5-10 minutes for the flavours to marry.

Chinese Chicken Hotpot

4-6 SERVINGS

*900 g (2 lb) chicken portions (thighs
and breasts would be best – a
whole chicken is too fatty for this
dish)*

FOR THE MARINADE

½ glass sherry

½ glass soy sauce

2 garlic cloves, finely chopped

*2.5 cm (1 inch) piece of fresh root
ginger, peeled and finely chopped*

2 tablespoons sesame oil

*1 teaspoon Szechuan peppercorns,
toasted and ground (see Note)
(you could substitute black
pepper)*

FOR THE HOTPOT

*125 g (4 oz) dried mushrooms (black
Chinese mushrooms are the
cheapest)*

sunflower oil, if needed

6 garlic cloves

*7.5 cm (3 inch) piece of fresh root
ginger, peeled and finely chopped*

*225 g (8 oz) fresh chestnuts, peeled
(see page 164), or dried chestnuts,
soaked overnight and drained*

4 star anise

*1 tablespoon Szechuan peppercorns,
toasted and ground (see Note)*

1 wine glass sherry

1 wine glass soy sauce

2 tablespoons sesame oil

Mix together all the marinade ingredients in a bowl, add the chicken
pieces and stir to coat. Leave to marinate for at least 1 hour (though a
day and night in the fridge will give even better results).

Soak the dried mushrooms in warm water for 30 minutes–1 hour,
then drain, reserving the water. Cut the mushrooms into bite-sized
pieces. Strain the soaking water to remove any grit, and set aside.

Drain the chicken from the marinade, reserving the marinade, and
put it in the bottom of a flameproof casserole. Heat gently until
browned, adding a very small dash of sunflower oil if you need it to
keep the pieces from sticking. When the chicken is nearly brown
enough, put in the garlic cloves and let them turn a little golden. Add
the ginger and the chestnuts and turn them until they are covered in the
fat. Put in the spices and let them fry for a few seconds, then add the
mushrooms. When all is hot, pour over the sherry, let it sizzle for a few
seconds, then add the marinade, the soy sauce and the water the mushrooms were soaked in. Put on a tight-fitting lid and cook in the oven at
150°C (300°F) mark 2 for 5 hours or at 180°C (350°F) mark 4 for 2
hours. Add the sesame oil about 5 minutes before the end of the cooking time.

N O T E : *To toast the Szechuan peppercorns, put them in a dry pan and heat gently, stirring, until they begin to give off their aroma. Remove from the heat, leave to cool, then grind in a mortar or strong bowl.*

Pork, Apple and Onion Hotpot

The secret of this excellent dish is slow cooking. This melts the pork fat which mingles with the apple and onion juices to make a rustic but highly savoury mélange.

4-6 SERVINGS

700 g (1½ lb) belly of pork rashers
700 g (1½ lb) large onions, sliced
700 g (1½ lb) firm but juicy apples, eg Bramleys or Cox's, peeled, cored and sliced

salt and pepper
450 g (1 lb) 'floury' potatoes, peeled and thinly sliced (optional)
butter (optional)

Cut the skin off the pork rashers, and cut them in half. Layer the onions, apple slices and pork pieces, in that order, in an ovenproof casserole. Sprinkle with salt and pepper as you go. Continue until all the ingredients are used up, ending with a layer of onion or apple. You can cap the dish with a layer of overlapping potato slices dotted with butter, if you like. Cover the dish with foil and bake in the oven at 180°C (350°F) mark 4 for 1 hour, then remove the foil and turn the heat down to 170°C (325°F) mark 3 for another hour. Serve with buttered carrots, more potatoes, or crisp-cooked buttered cabbage.

V A R I A T I O N : This is pretty good as it is, but you can add a little fresh thyme or savory, or a few slightly bruised juniper berries, for variety.

Brisket of Beef

Brisket is a humble cut of beef, inexpensive and fatty but, like many such, it rewards thoughtful cooking with a beefiness that makes much more expensive cuts taste pallid by comparison. It's the fat that does it; in this recipe it is slowly rendered out of the joint (you can pour it off, for dripping), leaving it succulent and full of flavour. This is one of my mother's recipes – plain English country food of the sort that is creeping back on to menus. She has a good, helpful butcher, and cooks the brisket in a tall brown pottery casserole with a lid.

8 SERVINGS

vegetable oil for frying	1-2 sprigs of fresh thyme (optional)
salt and pepper	1 garlic clove, slivered (optional)
mustard powder	1-2 tablespoons wine, cider or water
900 g-1.4 kg (2-3 lb) rolled and	
boned brisket	

Heat a little oil in a frying pan large enough to take the joint. Meanwhile, heat a deep pottery casserole in the oven at 170°C (325°F) mark 3. Mix salt, pepper and mustard powder together, and rub it into the meat firmly, pushing it down into the cracks. You can insert a sprig of thyme or two, or slivers of garlic, if you want. Put the brisket in the pan and turn until browned on all sides, top and bottom included. Stand the joint on its end in the casserole. Put the wine, cider or water into the pan, stir to scrape up residual bits of meat, and pour over the joint. Cover the casserole with foil or greaseproof paper to make a tighter seal, put on the lid and cook in the oven for 2-2½ hours, depending on weight.

After cooking, the meat will have shrunk, but be very tender and sitting in a pool of meat juices and hot fat. Pour this off into a cold bowl, let it settle for a few minutes (you can return the meat to the bottom of the oven), then spoon off the clear fat – keep it, naturally – and bubble up the remaining meat juices with a little more water, cider or wine, for a rich gravy, which needs no flour or other ingredients. Serve with baked potatoes, boiled carrots or spring greens and lots more freshly made mustard. Use the dripping to sauté leftover potatoes, or add a sprig of rosemary to it, leave it to solidify, then spread it on hot toast for a rustic snack.

Rice Pudding

It is surprising how few rice puddings taste the way they should – neither stodgy nor gritty, but tender, creamy and mellow. There is no mystery to making a successful rice pudding – it depends on using the right proportions of rice to milk, and long, slow cooking. The proportions given in this recipe are the same for all milk and cereal puddings.

4 SERVINGS

568 ml (1 pint) milk	a few drops of vanilla essence, or
2 tablespoons short-grain (pudding)	1 vanilla pod
rice	15 g (½ oz) butter
2-3 tablespoons sugar	

Butter a shallow ovenproof dish lightly. Pour in the milk, add the rice and sugar and stir to distribute them evenly. Add the vanilla essence or a vanilla pod and dot a few little pieces of butter on top. Cook in the oven at 170°C (325°F) mark 3.

After about 30 minutes, when a skin has formed on top, stir the skin into the pudding. Repeat this about an hour later. The pudding will be cooked in 2½ hours. If you are cooking something else in the oven at the same time, put the pudding on a lower shelf, the bottom shelf if the oven is hot.

VARIATION: An alternative way of cooking rice is to use the top of a double saucepan, cooking it for 3–4 hours over barely simmering water, until all the milk is absorbed. Use the same ingredients and proportions as for the method above. In the Middle East, rice cooked like this is mixed with thick, or whipped, cream and served very cold with a powdering of cinnamon.

Bread and Butter Pudding

Like most simple dishes, bread and butter pudding needs to be made with care. The slices of bread should be really thin, with the crusts removed – but don't give in to the temptation to use packed sliced bread unless you want the pudding to taste like wet flannel!

4-6 SERVINGS

6 thin slices of stale white bread,
    buttered
a handful of raisins or sultanas
5-6 tablespoons sugar

450 ml (¾ pint) milk
½ teaspoon vanilla essence
2 eggs, plus 1 extra yolk
a knob of butter

Cut the bread and butter into quarters or triangles. Arrange them in layers in an ovenproof dish, with a sprinkling of raisins or sultanas and sugar on each layer.

Put the milk and vanilla essence in a saucepan and heat gently until almost boiling. Beat the eggs and egg yolk in a bowl and mix with the heated milk. Pour this over the bread and butter. Some people believe in letting the pudding stand for 30 minutes or so before baking. Otherwise, sprinkle sugar over the top, dot with a little butter and bake in the oven at 170°C (325°F) mark 3 for 45 minutes–1 hour.

Equally good hot or cold, served plain or with cream.

Junket and Cream

Junket is such a simple, unpretentious pudding that it tends to be over-looked. Dressed up with banana purée (see below), it is quite nice enough to produce at a dinner party.

568 ml (1 pint) whole (silver-top) milk
about 2 teaspoons sugar
1 small teaspoon rennet

freshly grated nutmeg or ground cinnamon, to taste
150 ml (¼ pint) double cream

Heat the milk over a low heat until just tepid. Add the sugar (according to taste), stir well, pour into a shallow dish, stir in the rennet and leave to set. Pour on the cream and sprinkle with a little cinnamon or nutmeg before serving.

For a slightly more elaborate version, mash two ripe bananas until very soft and frothy, adding a little sugar. Put them in the bottom of the dish, pour the junket over and leave to set as before.

Polish Apple Charlotte

6-8 SERVINGS
900 g (2 lb) cooking apples
sugar, to taste
1 teaspoon grated lemon rind

a knob of butter
4 macaroons, crushed
about 2 tablespoons marmalade

Core, peel and slice the apples. Put them in a saucepan with a little water, sugar to taste and the lemon rind. Cook gently until soft, then sieve them into a baking dish and stir in the butter. Mix the crushed macaroons with enough marmalade to bind them together and spread over the apples. Bake in the oven at 180°C (350°F) mark 4 for 20 minutes. Serve with cream.

Spiced Apple Purée

Most apple purées are plain stewed apples given a hopeful and vigorous stir with a wooden spoon. The result is a watery mush. It takes a minute longer to convert this into the proper velvet-smooth consistency, but this minute is crucial.

4 SERVINGS

900 g (2 lb) cooking apples
4 cloves
a pinch of ground cinnamon

sugar to taste
25 g (1 oz) butter

Peel, core and slice the apples. Put them in a saucepan with the cloves, cinnamon and enough water to cover. Cook gently until the apples are soft, then add sugar to taste. Press the apple mixture through a fine sieve, removing the cloves. (The sieving is vital because it removes the little fibres and gives a smooth purée. Use a plastic sieve if possible.) Stir in the butter and leave to cool. Serve with cream.

Apple Pie

Serve hot, with cream, for pudding, or cold for tea.

6-8 SERVINGS

4 large cooking or firm eating apples
juice of 1 lemon
10 tablespoons self-raising flour
6 tablespoons caster sugar
4 tablespoons oil
a drop of vanilla essence
8 tablespoons milk
2 eggs

a pinch of salt
1 teaspoon ground cinnamon (more if
   you like)
sugar for dusting
50 g (2 oz) butter
25 g (1 oz) walnuts, almonds or
   hazelnuts, roughly chopped
   (optional)

Peel, core and slice the apples and pour the lemon juice over them to stop them browning. Grease a medium-sized flan dish or cake tin.

Put the flour and sugar in a bowl, make a well in the centre and add the oil, vanilla essence, milk, eggs, salt and cinnamon to taste. Beat well to incorporate all the flour and form a smooth, thick batter. Alternatively, put all the ingredients in a food mixer and mix to a batter. Pour the batter into the prepared flan dish or cake tin.

Arrange the slices of apple on top of the batter, in a haphazard way or with pâtisserie smartness, as you like. Scatter a little more sugar, little lumps of butter and the broken nuts, if using, all over the pie and bake it in the oven at 200–220°C (400–425°F) mark 6–7 for almost 1 hour or until the pie is twice the size and golden.

Apricot Fool

Apricots are quite a reasonable price towards the end of the summer, and they make excellent fool. If you can't run to 300 ml (10 fl oz) cream, use the smaller amount and add the beaten white of an egg.

4 SERVINGS

450 g (1 lb) apricots
3-4 tablespoons sugar

200-300 ml (7-10 fl oz) double cream, whipped

Cut the apricots in half and take out the stones. Crack open four or five of the stones with a hammer and extract the kernels. (The kernels add an extra something to the flavour so this little effort is worth making.)

Put the apricot halves, kernels and sugar into an ovenproof dish, add just enough water to cover them and bake in the oven at 180°C (350°F) mark 4 until the apricots are soft. Remove the kernels and rub the apricots through a sieve into a bowl. Fold in the whipped cream. Taste to see if the fool is sweet enough and add a little more sugar if necessary. Set aside to cool.

Batter Pudding

6-8 SERVINGS

3 eggs
200 g (7 oz) plain flour
a pinch of salt
300 ml (½ pint) milk

15 g (½ oz) butter
4 tablespoons golden syrup
a dash of rum or brandy (optional)

Beat the eggs lightly, then sift in the flour and salt and stir together. Gradually add the milk, stirring all the time. Leave to stand for 1-2 hours.

Butter a baking tin and pour in the batter. Dot with butter and bake in the oven at 230°C (450°F) mark 8 for 15 minutes, then turn the oven down to 200°C (400°F) mark 6 and cook for a further 15-30 minutes or until the batter is risen and golden. In a small but heavy-based saucepan over a gentle heat, stir the golden syrup with a little water and a dash of rum or brandy, if using. When this is melted and thin, pour it over each person's slice of hot pudding.

56

Padding

This chapter deals with the art (or science) of stretching small quantities of food (and money) a bit further. Leftovers are part of the story, but the emphasis here is not so much on what bits and pieces you have to work with as on various ways of expanding them into a solid meal. This is where the idea of padding comes in. Rice and pasta are two examples of padding which need little introduction from me. But there are other less familiar ones – batters, pastry, suetcrust, pulses, polenta, pizza bases – which paupers ought to know about. The reason being, of course, that they are dazzlingly cheap and versatile. A short-crust pastry flan case, for instance. This costs next to nothing to make. Onions, butter, flour and a little cream turn it into a savoury meal for two, or first course for four. Similarly, a trifling outlay on batter makes a few sausages into a meal for three or four people. A lot of suet-crust and a little jam gives you a roly-poly pudding to silence a party of hungry schoolboys. 450 g (1 lb) haricot beans, some belly of pork and a few other odds and ends add up to a hearty dish of Pork and Beans (see page 41) which will feed six comfortably.

No Victorian housewife would have needed reminding of these basic principles of economical cookery. But, with the current craze for high-protein, low-calorie diets, I think many of these padding foods have fallen into disrepute, as being fattening, indigestible and some-how unwholesome. And yet about a quarter of the nation's grocery bills goes on biscuits, and the same people who quail at the sight of a suet pudding will cheerfully consume mountains of crisps, cereals and chocolate bars. The point to remember, I think, is that a normal diet should strike a balance between starch, protein and vitamin foods. The padding foods in this chapter are high in carbohydrates, but this only becomes a bad thing, dietetically speaking, if you eat nothing else. A thick lentil soup, followed by steak and kidney pudding and mashed potatoes and a fruit pie, would be too much. Solid dishes need to be balanced by salads, green vegetables, light fruit puddings, thin soups.

Another point I would like to make about the padding foods men-tioned in this chapter is that they are not tediously slow and com-plicated, or difficult, to make. A lot of people are put off attempting pastry, for instance, by the mystique which has grown up round the subject – all that talk about 'light hands', correct temperatures, propor-tions – which is a pity because pastry-making is a simple process and only requires a few trial runs to be reasonably foolproof. (Shortcrust and suetcrust, that is. I have deliberately excluded the more elaborate varieties like puff and flaky pastry.) Once you are familiar with the procedure you will find it takes about 5 minutes to make pastry, or bat-ters, a couple of minutes with a rolling pin to produce home-made breadcrumbs.

Rice

It is astonishing how much disagreement reigns over the best way of boiling rice. This may be because it has only comparatively recently been grown in Europe, and a certain mystery still clings to its pre-paration. Having tried some of the more complicated methods, I am pleased to say that the easiest and quickest also gives the best results.

The best rice for boiling is the long-grain or Patna variety. Short-grain rice is suitable for puddings where the grains need to be highly absorbent. I generally use rather more rice than specified – just under 225 g (8 oz) for two people. Leftovers can be used up in salads, or com-bined with other ingredients in stuffings.

Bring a large pan of salted water to the boil and tip in the rice. Boil fast for about 12 minutes, though you should try the rice before this time as it may cook more quickly. When cooked, rice should be tender, but not too soft. Packaged rice will give an approximate cook-ing time on the packet. Drain in a colander or sieve and rinse with boil-ing water to wash off any glutinous starch. Alternatively, boil the rice for only 6-7 minutes, then to dry off and separate the grains, you can either return the rice to the pan after draining it, and leave it covered over a very low heat for 5-10 minutes, stirring once or twice with a fork to loosen the grains, or (which is marginally easier) you can pour it into a shallow ovenproof dish, cover it and put it in the oven for 10 minutes or so.

Rice Salad

Cold rice can be mixed with a great variety of bits and pieces and turned into a successful salad. Any of the following suggestions can be used in varying combinations, according to what is available: canned or fresh crab, shrimps, cooked mussels, cooked chicken, ham, garlic sausage, hard-boiled egg, cucumber, tomatoes (skinned), raw onion, cooked peas, spring onions, raw mushrooms, green pepper, green beans, beetroot, raisins, sultanas, capers, raw apple, carrot, mild cheese. You will probably be able to think of many more. The main thing is to try and balance the textures and flavours pleasantly – something crisp, something soft, something sharp, something sweet, etc. And dice or chop the ingredients quite small; rice with large lumps of stuff buried in it looks sloppy and faintly sinister.

When you have combined your chosen ingredients with the rice, season it well with salt and pepper or paprika, moisten liberally with a mild vinaigrette – more oily than vinegary – or thin mayonnaise, and, if possible, sprinkle some chopped parsley, or other herbs, on top.

Hot Savoury Rice

There are two ways of preparing dishes of savoury rice. The easiest, and I think safest for non-Italians, is to boil the rice and cook up the other ingredients separately, giving them a few minutes together in the pan or oven to merge the flavours just at the end. The other way, more properly the risotto or paella method, is to cook all the ingredients to-gether, first frying the rice, and then adding boiling liquid (stock, water, wine or a mixture of the three) gradually, together with scraps of meat, fish, chicken, vegetables or whatever, until the rice is tender. The second method does produce a richer dish, with a moist creamy texture, when correctly cooked. But it requires more judgement and concentration on the part of the cook if it is not to turn into an un-appetising sludge, or worse still, a mass of gritty, undercooked rice. You do also need a really good heavy cast-iron or flameproof earthen-ware dish to cook it in.

59

My advice is, practise making risottos or paellas in small quantities, for private consumption, but avoid the common mistake of serving them up as a cheap omnibus meal for dinner guests until you are confident of getting the right results. In the meantime, the other method, or the method used in making Suleiman's Pilaff (see below), a compromise between the two, will save a lot of nervous strain.

Suleiman's Pilaff

An excellent way of using up small bits and pieces of cooked lamb left over from a joint. The rice is fried before boiling to make it richer.

4-6 SERVINGS

dripping or olive oil for frying
450 g (1 lb) long-grain rice
1.1 litres (2 pints) boiling water
2-3 onions, chopped
2 garlic cloves, chopped
4 fresh tomatoes, chopped, or 230 g
  (8 oz) can of chopped tomatoes

1 tablespoon currants
1 tablespoon sultanas
a pinch of dried thyme or rosemary
salt and pepper
125-175 g (4-6 oz) lean cooked
  lamb, diced

Melt a good lump of dripping, or heat 3 tablespoons olive oil in a heavy-based saucepan and fry the rice gently, stirring, until it begins to look transparent. Pour the boiling water over the rice and boil fast, uncovered, for about 12 minutes or until the rice is tender. Strain and return to the pan, cover and leave over a very low heat.

Meanwhile, fry the other ingredients in oil or dripping, starting with the onions and garlic and adding the tomatoes, dried fruit and herbs, when these are golden. Season generously and simmer gently until thick. Add the diced meat towards the end – too much cooking is liable to toughen it.

Stir the meat mixture into the rice, adding more dripping if you think it needs it. Cook over a gentle heat for a few minutes longer and serve.

In the Middle East a savoury pilaff would be served with yogurt or soured cream stirred into it. If that idea does not appeal to you, try serving a salad of thinly sliced cucumber dressed with a little yogurt or soured cream and a few finely chopped mint leaves, along with the pilaff. Alternatively, a salad made with oranges and onions would be a refreshing combination.

Risi e Bisi

This is a beloved first course in Italy, served wetter than most risottos, though the method holds good for any risotto. I think this is really so wonderful with fresh new peas you may as well cook something else when they are not in season.

4 SERVINGS

900 g (2 lb) young peas
1.7 litres (3 pints) thin chicken stock
50 g (2 oz) butter
2 tablespoons olive oil
1 onion, sliced
*2 rashers of bacon, de-rinded and
  sliced*

*450 g (1 lb) easy-cook long-grain or
  arborio rice*
salt and pepper
grated Parmesan cheese, to serve

Pod the peas and put the pods in a saucepan with the stock. Bring to the boil, then reduce the heat and simmer over a very low heat.

Meanwhile, heat the butter and oil in a deep, heavy-based frying pan large enough to hold the finished risotto, and add the onion and bacon. Heat gently until the fat runs out of the bacon, then fry until the onions are translucent and tender, but not brown. Stir in the rice and when it becomes translucent, stir in the peas. After a second, pour in some of the hot stock (without pods) and season with salt and pepper. Cook until the stock has been absorbed, then add a little more stock and cook again. Continue adding the stock, a cupful at a time, so that the rice and peas remain surrounded by moisture, but never invisible under the stock. Stir the mixture occasionally with a wooden spoon, so that it cannot burn on the bottom, but try not to mash it with constant stirring. When the rice is tender, taste and season again if it needs it. Serve with grated Parmesan.

Stir-Fried Rice with Beef

The rice must be cooked (see page 58), drained and cold. Yesterday's rice is best.

4-6 SERVINGS

4 tablespoons soy sauce
8 tablespoons peanut (groundnut) oil
salt and pepper
a pinch of Chinese five-spice powder
    (optional)
450 g (1 lb) minced beef
6 spring onions

2 large eggs
6 garlic cloves, chopped
1 cm (½ inch) piece of fresh root
    ginger, peeled and chopped
900 g (2 lb) cooked long-grain rice
1 tablespoon sesame oil

Mix the soy sauce, 1 tablespoon peanut oil, a pinch of salt, plenty of pepper and the five-spice powder (if using) in a bowl. Add the mince, stir to coat, then leave to marinate for about 1 hour, stirring quite vigorously from time to time.

Slice the spring onions, including the green parts, and arrange the green and white pieces in two separate piles. Beat the eggs with ½ tablespoon peanut oil.

Heat a wok or large frying pan gradually until it begins to smoke. Pour in 5 or 6 tablespoons of the peanut oil and swirl it around in the pan. Put in the garlic, stir it about and, after a moment, add the ginger and the white parts of the spring onions. Stir again, then put in the beef, stirring all the time. When it is browned, pour in the beaten egg, then the rice and toss for 1-2 minutes or until the rice is hot and the meat mixture dispersed evenly through it. Pour the sesame oil down the side of the pan into the mixture. Add the green parts of the spring onions, stir again and serve.

Barley

Barley is commonly used in small quantities to provide a nutty taste and pleasant texture in soups and stews.

Barley Kail Soup

An old Scots cottage recipe, and highly economical.

4-6 SERVINGS

50 g (2 oz) pearl barley
1.1 litres (2 pints) Simple Stock (see page 21)
450 g (1 lb) kale, trimmed of coarse stalks and finely shredded

3 leeks, sliced
salt and pepper

Put the barley and stock in a large saucepan and simmer for about 45 minutes or until the barley is tender, skimming off any scum which rises to the surface. Add the kale and leeks, and simmer until the vegetables are tender, adding salt and pepper as necessary.

Oats

It is quite a good idea to have a packet of rolled oats around, even if you do not eat porridge. They are useful for coating herring and mackerel before frying, as the Scots do. A spoonful or two can be used to thicken soups and stews.

 ## Porridge

Porridge oats – not the instant type – are greatly improved by steeping overnight in milk before cooking. This brings out all their flavour and gives a creamy texture. The Scots name for this used to be Crowdie-Mowdie. They also used to steam the oats for 2 hours, but I think that is a refinement which can be disregarded.

1 SERVING

25 g (1 oz) porridge oats
175 ml (6 fl oz) milk

a pinch of salt

Mix all the ingredients together and leave overnight. To cook, bring the milk and oats slowly to simmering point and cook gently for 5–8 minutes, or until the porridge thickens.

Scots Fried Herrings

Herrings are very good rolled in oats, and fried. They can be cooked whole, or split, boned and flattened.

2 SERVINGS

2 large or 4 small herrings	25 g (1 oz) dripping or butter and
salt and pepper	½ tablespoon oil
25 g (1 oz) porridge oats	lemon wedges, to serve

Wipe the fish carefully, then season them with salt and pepper. Sprinkle the oats on a sheet of kitchen paper and toss the fish in them until well coated. Heat the dripping or butter and oil in a frying pan and, when smoking hot, put in the herrings and fry until brown on both sides. Whole herrings will take 7–10 minutes; split herrings will take 5 minutes. Serve with lemon wedges and boiled potatoes.

Millet

Millet is a small, sweetish grain, like a seed pearl with a tiny black spot on it to look at. It should be white rather than yellow – yellow millet is a bit old, and takes longer to soften. It makes a pleasant change from rice, burghul, etc., eaten as an accompaniment, or added to stuffings or salads. I like to boil it up first, then bake it a while in a low oven with butter and chopped chives, or a few currants or raisins. The volume of the cooked grain is about three times the raw; it expands less than rice.

3-4 SERVINGS

125 g (4 oz) millet	salt and pepper
a knob of butter	

Wash the grain by running cold water through it briefly. Put it into a large saucepan of boiling water and boil for 25 minutes or until the grains have burst and swollen, without becoming mushy. If still on the gritty side, boil for another 10 minutes or so, until just tender. Strain off the water and turn the millet into an ovenproof dish. Stir in the butter, seasoning and any additions you fancy, and cook in the oven at 170°C (325°F) mark 3 for 15 minutes.

Burghul with Raisins and Nuts

Both the raisins and nuts are optional, since burghul alone has a sweet-ish, mealy taste which is quite addictive. However, they dress up the bowl for party purposes. I prefer the texture of burghul after steaming, anyway, though swelling with cold water is supposed to be adequate for salads like tabbouleh, since the cracked wheat is pre-cooked.

6 SERVINGS

450 g (1 lb) burghul
a good handful of raisins, currants or
  sultanas
a squeeze of orange or lemon juice
  (optional)

50 g (2 oz) butter
1 tablespoon oil
salt and pepper
50 g (2 oz) flaked almonds or pine
  nuts, lightly toasted

Put the burghul in a bowl, cover with cold water and leave to soak for 30 minutes. Soak the dried fruit in a little warm water, with a squeeze of orange or lemon juice added, if used.

Tip the soaked burghul into a round sieve that fits over a saucepan. Bring about 2.5 cm (1 inch) of water to the boil in the saucepan and place the sieve over the top. Loosely cover with a lid and cook for 10 minutes. Fork up the burghul to aerate it, then steam for another 10–15 minutes, making sure the water does not boil dry. Turn the burghul into a warmed serving dish and stir in the soaked fruit. Heat the butter and oil together in a saucepan and pour over the burghul, fluffing it up with a fork. Season to taste with a little salt and pepper. Finally, scatter toasted nuts on top and serve.

Buckwheat Kasha

4-6 SERVINGS

450 g (1 lb) husked buckwheat grain   *salt*
1 litre (1¾ pints) boiling water

Wash the buckwheat, removing any husks or unhusked grains. Put the buckwheat in a frying pan without any fat, and heat gently, stirring and shaking all the time, until it begins to pop and is roasted. Transfer to an ovenproof dish large enough to allow plenty of space for the kasha to swell. Add the water, season with salt, stir well, cover and cook in the oven at 180°C (350°F) mark 4, with the dish standing in a deep baking tray or roasting tin full of water, for about 45 minutes or until the grains are soft. Serve with meat, game or sausages.

Pulses

A whole range of dried vegetables comes under this heading – haricot beans, lentils, split peas, chickpeas, butter beans, etc. They are all cheap, can be usefully alternated with fresh vegetables, especially in winter, and form the basis of several good dishes in their own right. Incidentally, even dried vegetables deteriorate with time, so if you are stuck with a pan of beans which refuse to soften after hours of boiling, the chances are that they are antiques and have been kept too long.

All these vegetables should be soaked before cooking, unless specific instructions to the contrary are given on the packet. This cuts down the cooking time considerably and makes them more tender. Soaking overnight in tepid water will be enough for all of them.

To cook pulses, drain off the water they were soaked in. Pick out any blackened-looking vegetables, and any grit which may have found its way in, and put them in a large saucepan. Add cold water to more than cover, a sliced onion, a carrot, a clove of garlic, and salt and pepper to taste, and bring slowly to the boil. Boil rapidly for 10 minutes (especially important for kidney beans, red and black, and soya beans), then reduce the heat, cover and simmer until tender. The initial fast boiling destroys toxins present in some dried pulses. Most pulses need 1-2 hours' cooking, depending on quality and age. Split peas and lentils take less time than the others; chickpeas may need up to 6 hours. Never add salt until the pulses are tender because it tends to toughen them.

If you want to serve the pulses as they come, they are now ready to be drained and dished up with a dash of oil, a lump of butter and a sprinkling of parsley or grated cheese stirred in. For other ideas, see the following recipes.

Hummus

A blender or food processor makes this recipe an easy task. It's possible to do it with a food mill or even in a mortar, but not unless you have plenty of time on your hands. Chickpeas take such a long time to soak and cook (and a pauper must remember fuel costs), it would seem sensible to boil more than you need for this recipe (most packets contain 450 g/1 lb) and use the rest for something else – the soup on page 113, for example, or Pasta and Chickpea Salad (see page 103). Tahina (sesame seed paste) is always included in an authentic hummus, but it is expensive so if you don't want to pay for it or can't find it in your shops, the chickpeas will manage deliciously on their own.

8 SERVINGS

200 g (7 oz) chickpeas	75 ml (3 fl oz) olive oil
salt	1-2 tablespoons tahina (optional)
4 garlic cloves	cayenne pepper
juice of 1 lemon	

Soak the chickpeas in cold water overnight. Drain the chickpeas, put them in a large saucepan, cover them with fresh cold water and bring to the boil. Boil rapidly for 20 minutes, then reduce the heat, cover and simmer for 2–4 hours or until the chickpeas are tender, seasoning with salt towards the end of cooking. Drain the chickpeas, reserving the cooking water.

Put the whole garlic cloves in a mixing bowl or blender with a cupful of the chickpeas. Mash or purée the chickpeas, a cupful at a time, pouring in the lemon juice and some of the cooking liquor and a dribble or so of olive oil as you go. Mix in the tahina. When the whole is smooth and creamy, pour it into a bowl, sprinkle with cayenne pepper and dribble over a little olive oil. Hummus is usually served with pitta bread, but hot toast is just as good.

 ## Split Pea Soup

This is real pauper's food.

4-6 SERVINGS

1 onion, studded with 2 cloves	1 ham or gammon bone
1 bay leaf	225 g (8 oz) split peas
1 sprig of fresh thyme, or a pinch of dried	1.1 litres (2 pints) water
	salt and black pepper

Put the onion and cloves, the bay leaf and thyme in a large saucepan with the ham or gammon bone and split peas. Pour over the water and simmer for about 1 hour or until the peas are soft enough to mash. Remove the bone, onion and herbs, season with salt and pepper and serve the soup piping hot.

Haricot Bean Salad

Boiled haricot beans make a pleasant salad which can be eaten on its own, as an hors d'oeuvre, or with cold meat, salami, ham, etc. This is a handy way of using up any leftover boiled beans.

2 SERVINGS

125 g (4 oz) dried haricot beans, soaked and cooked (see page 66)
French Dressing (see page 169)
salt and black pepper

1 onion, finely chopped
1 tablespoon finely chopped fresh parsley

Drain the beans, preferably while still warm and season to taste with French dressing, salt and black pepper. Stir in the onion and parsley.

VARIATIONS: Lentils and chickpeas are also good served like this. Add some garlic to the chickpeas, and a little pounded anchovy to the lentils.

Lentils and Anchovies

An oddly successful mixture, this, with an elusive, smoky flavour, not in the least fishy. Well worth trying when you want a cheap but nourishing dish. It can be eaten on its own, with a crisp green salad and lots of black pepper, or with a halved hard–boiled egg added to each helping. The lentils must be the brown variety, which can be bought at most health food stores and good supermarkets.

4 SERVINGS

225 g (8 oz) brown lentils
1 onion, roughly chopped
50 g (2 oz) can of anchovy fillets, drained
75 g (3 oz) butter

2 garlic cloves, crushed
salt and black pepper
4 hard-boiled eggs, halved (optional)

Soak the lentils in cold water for 1-2 hours. Remove any lentils and tiny stalks which float to the top. Drain the lentils and transfer them to a large saucepan, add the onion and cover with fresh cold water. Bring to the boil slowly and simmer for 1-1½ hours or until the lentils are tender but not cooked to a mush. Drain in a colander.

Meanwhile, mash the anchovy fillets to a pulp with a wooden spoon. Melt 25 g (1 oz) butter over a low heat in a heavy-based saucepan or flameproof serving dish and stir in the lentil and onion mixture, together with the garlic. After a few minutes, when the lentils are heated through, stir in the pounded anchovies. Cook gently for a few minutes longer, stirring in the rest of the butter, a knob at a time. Add salt and pepper to taste. Serve, with or without the hard-boiled eggs.

N O T E : *This dish can be reheated by adding a little more butter and warming it, covered, in the oven at 170°C (325°F) mark 3 for 30 minutes.*

Slow-Cooked Spiced Beans

The best equipment for this would be a deep, narrow earthenware pot with a tight-fitting lid. Failing that, any heavy casserole will do that is not too broad-based.

8 SERVINGS

a large bunch of fresh parsley, finely chopped
4 garlic cloves, finely chopped
1 teaspoon ground cinnamon
1 teaspoon ground cloves
1 teaspoon ground mace

1 teaspoon ground black pepper
a piece of pork rind (perhaps from a hand of pork), cut into strips
450 g (1 lb) white haricot beans, soaked overnight

Put the parsley, garlic and spices in a mortar or strong bowl and pound together with a pestle or the end of a rolling pin until they form a paste. Spread the pieces of pork rind with this mixture, roll them up and put them in the bottom of a deep, narrow casserole. Drain the beans and put them on top. Pour in enough water to cover the ingredients by 5 cm (2 inches), put the lid on and cook in the bottom oven of an Aga/Raeburn-type of oven overnight, or at 140-150°C (275-300°F) mark 1-2 for 5-6 hours.

Butter Beans

An excellent dish to serve with roast lamb.

4 SERVINGS

450 g (1 lb) dried butter beans
a pinch of salt
150 ml (¼ pint) olive oil
2 garlic cloves, crushed
2 teaspoons tomato purée

plenty of black pepper
2 leaves of fresh sage or a sprig of
    fresh rosemary, or a pinch of dried
4 sun-dried tomatoes, chopped small
    (optional)

Soak the beans overnight, or for at least 4 hours, in cold water. Drain the beans and put them in a large saucepan. Cover with fresh cold water and bring to the boil. Boil rapidly for 10 minutes, then reduce the heat, cover and simmer until just tender. This may take anything from 30 minutes to 2 hours, depending on the youth of the beans. Salt the water and cook for 1 minute more, then drain.

Meanwhile, mix the olive oil, garlic, tomato purée, pepper, herbs and sun-dried tomatoes, if using, in a screw-topped jar. Screw the lid on and shake hard. Pour over the hot beans and serve immediately. It is the cold olive oil hitting the hot beans that makes this so good. If you want to prepare the beans beforehand, cook them until they are just ready, then leave them in their water. When the time comes to eat them, heat them up, drain and dress them.

Pease Pudding

4-6 SERVINGS

450 g (1 lb) dried peas or split peas
50 g (2 oz) butter

1 egg, beaten
salt and pepper

If they are likely to be a bit old, soak the peas for 1-2 hours in plenty of cold water, then drain them and put them in a large saucepan with fresh water. Bring to the boil, then reduce the heat, cover and simmer for 1-2 hours or until tender. Drain the peas and purée them by passing them through a sieve or food mill, or by processing them in a blender or food processor. Stir in the butter and egg, season generously with salt and pepper and pour the mixture into a buttered pudding basin or fairly high-sided gratin dish. Cover with foil, or greaseproof paper and foil, and stand in a saucepan of water. Cover the pan and steam for 1 hour. Turn the pudding out of the basin and serve with pork or poultry, or on its own with chips. Any leftover pease pudding can be sliced when cold and fried or grilled rather like polenta (see page 80).

[10] Shortcrust Pastry

Making pastry is one of those things which seems dishearteningly complicated if you have never tried it, and childishly simple once you have. Shortcrust pastry, particularly, is quick and easy to make, versatile and reasonably foolproof – no pastry, as expert cooks will tell you, is 100 per cent foolproof. However, if you stick to the directions, it will always be edible even if it falls short of crisp perfection.

Many cookbook recipes for pastry-making are bogged down in theory. The more confidently you tackle it, I find, the better it turns out (your hands are likely to be cooler for one thing) so I shall give the instructions first and diagnose briefly a few of the things that can go wrong afterwards.

MAKES ENOUGH TO LINE ONE 20-23 CM (8-9 INCH) FLAN
DISH, OR COVER AN AVERAGE-SIZED PIE

175 g (6 oz) plain flour	*1 egg yolk*
a pinch of salt	*1-2 tablespoons water*
1 tablespoon sugar (for a sweet pie)	*a squeeze of lemon juice*
100 g (3½ oz) butter	

Sift the flour, salt and sugar, if using, together into a large mixing bowl. Make a well in the centre. Put in the butter and start cutting it into the flour with a knife. The idea is to break the butter into tiny pieces while working in as much flour as possible. When the knife seems to have done what it can, use your fingertips to rub the mixture together until the butter has absorbed all the loose flour and the particles are the size of breadcrumbs (fresh not dried crumbs). *Don't* overdo this stage to be on the safe side – pastry is better handled too little than too much.

Beat the egg yolk with the water and stir it into the crumbs with your knife. Add a squeeze of lemon juice to make the dough more pliable. Gather the sticky mess together with your fingertips and work lightly until it sticks together in a lump and some of the stickiness has gone.

Put the pastry dough on a plate in a cool place, or in the fridge, to rest for 1-2 hours before use. The point of this is to make the dough less tough and less liable to shrink in cooking.

To roll out the dough, flour the table top and the rolling pin (or milk bottle), and dust a little flour over the lump of pastry itself if it still feels very sticky. Roll out lightly but firmly until it is just under 5 mm (¼ inch) thick. If holes appear, tear off a patch, moisten the edges with milk, and iron over the hole with your rolling pin, sprinkling on a little more flour.

Lift the pastry sheet gently off the work surface – I usually slide a long knife blade underneath because it often sticks in places. Lay it over the flan tin and ease it in to fit the tin with your fingertips, taking care not to stretch it. Press it firmly down once it is in place – if you grease the tin lightly first the pastry will stick more obediently. Prick the bottom here and there with a fork. Roll the rolling pin over the top of the tin to trim off the extra pastry.

The next stage depends on whether your pastry is to cook with the filling, or separately. If the former, it is ready for the filling. If the latter (this is called baking 'blind'), cut a circle or strips of greaseproof paper to cover the bottom, then put in a cupful of uncooked dried beans. (Rice or crusts will do if you have no beans.) Put the flan in the top part of an oven preheated to 200°C (400°F) mark 6 and bake for 20 minutes. Remove the paper and beans and return to the oven for another 5–7 minutes. The pastry shell will now be golden brown, crisp and ready either to take a hot filling or to be left to cool and stored in an airtight container.

Some recipes only require the pastry to be partly prebaked, in which case there is no need to use the beans and paper.

If you are using the pastry to *cover* a pie, roll it out a little thicker, and put an eggcup in the pie dish to support the pastry (if the area is fairly large). The pie will look more elegant if you cut a long strip of pastry, moisten it on both sides with milk or water, and press it round the rim of the pie dish, before laying on the pastry cover. You can then go round the edge with a fork, dipped in milk, to give a ribbed effect and press the two layers firmly together. Make a few cuts in the pastry to let out steam. Odd bits of pastry can be cut into flower and leaf shapes and stuck over the pie with a spot of milk. Brush over the whole surface with milk or beaten egg yolk to colour it attractively and bake as directed.

NOTES:

1 *The recipe given above is for a rich shortcrust. For greater economy, you can use half butter, half margarine; all margarine; or half butter, half lard. Some people swear by the one, some by the other, but I think butter tastes nicer and the extra cost is negligible. For eating cold, however, margarine makes a*

lighter-textured pastry. You can dispense with the egg yolk, in which case use a little more water.

2 If the pastry comes out hard and tough, you used too much water. If it is crumbly, too much fat. If soggy, it has had too much handling or been cooked initially at too low a temperature. Preheating the oven is important.

3 If things still go wrong, check that you are making pastry under the right conditions – everything, from room temperature to your hands, should be as cool as possible. Cool your hands by rinsing under a cold tap and drying, and make the pastry if possible in the morning before the kitchen heats up. Above all, don't worry – try it a couple more times and it will come right.

Alsatian Onion Tart

An excellent recipe for the end of the week, when you are running out of cash and/or ideas. All you need is lots of onions, butter, shortcrust pastry and a couple of eggs. The filling is very tasty and the tart can be eaten hot, lukewarm or cold.

2-4 SERVINGS

one quantity Shortcrust Pastry (see page 71)
900 g (2 lb) onions, chopped
a large knob of butter
1-2 tablespoons plain flour

salt and black pepper
2 eggs, beaten
2 tablespoons single cream (optional)
2 tablespoons grated Cheddar cheese (optional)

Roll out the pastry and use to line a 20-23 cm (8-9 inch) flan tin (see page 72). Put the onions in a saucepan with a little water, and cook over a low heat until soft and tender. Add the butter and leave to stew for a few minutes longer, then take them off the heat and add just enough flour to bind them. Season with salt and pepper, and add the eggs and 1 tablespoon cream, if using, to make a thick mush. Spread this mixture in the flan tin, spoon the remaining cream or the grated cheese over the top and bake in the oven at 220°C (425°F) mark 7 for 20 minutes, then lower the heat to 190°C (375°F) mark 5 and continue cooking for 45 minutes–1 hour or until the pastry is crisp and the top nicely browned.

A plain green salad goes well with this. No other vegetables.

Suetcrust Pastry

Suetcrust is made in much the same way as shortcrust, using beef suet instead of butter or margarine. One useful point about it is that it can be used either for steamed puddings, like steak and kidney pudding, or baked as in jam roly-poly. Properly made, it is light and melting, and is associated with some of the best traditional English dishes.

MAKES ENOUGH TO LINE A 900 ML (1½ PINT) PUDDING BASIN

225 g (8 oz) self-raising flour, or
   plain flour and 1 teaspoon baking
   powder
a pinch of salt

½ tablespoon sugar (for a sweet
   pudding)
125 g (4 oz) shredded beef suet

Sift the flour, salt and sugar, if using, together. Add the suet, rubbing it in lightly with the fingertips for 1 minute. Gradually add enough water to make a light, spongy dough. Knead this lightly into a smooth ball on a floured board, roll out and use at once.

VARIATION: For an extra light, spongy dough, replace 50 g (2 oz) flour with 50 g (2 oz) fresh white breadcrumbs.

 ## Baked Apple Pudding

4-5 SERVINGS

50 g (2 oz) butter, softened
juice of 2 lemons and a little grated
   lemon rind
125 g (4 oz) soft brown sugar

1 quantity Suetcrust Pastry (see
   above)
550 g (1¼ lb) apples, peeled, cored
   and sliced

Cream the butter, lemon juice and brown sugar together and put it in the bottom of a greased 900 ml (1½ pint) pudding basin. Roll out the suetcrust pastry and use it to line the bottom and sides of the pudding basin, covering the butter/sugar mixture and leaving an overhang round the sides. Lay the apples together with the grated lemon rind and 2 tablespoons water on the crust. Fold over the edges to cover, and seal. Bake the pudding in the oven at 190°C (375°F) mark 5 until brown, then lower the heat to 150°C (300°F) mark 2 to finish cooking, which will take about 2 hours in all.

To serve, turn the pudding out on to a plate. The sugar and butter mixture will have turned to a lemony sauce which will run out over the top of the pudding. Serve with more sugar and cream.

 ## Plough Pudding

Suetcrust pastry, steamed or baked, is, I believe, one of the great English inventions, a homely native alternative to the more elegant pastries and yeast doughs of European culinary tradition. Though hardly suitable for a low-cholesterol diet, I find the resulting crust more digestible and less cloyingly rich than butter-based alternatives. Interestingly, suetcrust is creeping back on to metropolitan menus. This savoury roly-poly is a true peasant dish, with many variants, like green hawthorn buds instead of sage. What all the variations have in common is a thrifty proportion of tasty filling to substantial roly-poly crust. It is not the suet dish I would try out on visiting foreigners, but it makes hearty family eating. Get the best quality sausagemeat, ie pure meat sausages stripped of their skins. The pink pappy stuff offered by some butchers is revolting.

4-6 SERVINGS

225 g (8 oz) plain flour
125 g (4 oz) shredded beef suet
salt and black pepper
2 onions, chopped
125 g (4 oz) streaky bacon, de-rinded and chopped

1 tablespoon chopped fresh sage and/or parsley
2 tablespoons soft brown sugar
125-225 g (4-8 oz) pure pork sausagemeat
1 tablespoon mustard powder

Mix the flour, suet and a little salt and pepper in a bowl, and add enough cold water to make a firm dough. Roll out on a floured surface to make a rectangle about 1 cm (½ inch) thick. Mix the onion, bacon, herbs and sugar with the sausagemeat and spread evenly over the suet-crust. Season well, then roll up into a sausage shape. Roll this securely in a well-floured tea towel, tying the ends with string, and plunge into a large pan of boiling water. Cook over a moderate heat for just over 2 hours. Unroll the pudding, put it in a baking dish and bake in the oven at 190°C (375°F) mark 5 for about 30 minutes or until lightly browned. Serve with mustard, a sharp fruit jelly, and cabbage, greens or carrots.

Batter

Batter is one of the small miracles of cookery – how that pallid liquid is metamorphosed into a puffy golden pillow-crust is a mystery I hope never to have explained to me. As sheer padding, batter is unbeatable value. Try the Toad-in-the-Hole recipe and see.

As I have given the batter-making procedure in some detail in the recipe for Toad-in-the-Hole (see overleaf) I will not go into it here. A point to keep in mind when making batter, though, is always to bring it into contact with high heat – whether you are baking it in the oven, or frying it in deep fat. (Fritters can be fried in shallow fat but not so successfully.) This makes it light and ungreasy. In the case of fritters, drain them on crumpled absorbent kitchen paper for a minute before eating. If you wish, you may leave the batter to stand for an hour or so before using.

 Toad-in-the-Hole

Not a dish for sophisticates, but an excellent way of stretching half a pound of chipolatas into a solid meal for four people. Children, especially, love it. If you have time, I suggest braising the sausages in the oven at 180°C (350°F) mark 4 for 45 minutes with a little stock, gravy or butter and a dash of Worcestershire sauce, to encourage them to sweat out some of their lye, and remove that raw pink appearance. Drain them on absorbent kitchen paper to remove excess fat.

4 SERVINGS
125 g (4 oz) plain flour   *300 ml (½ pint) milk*
salt   *a little butter or dripping*
2 eggs   *225 g (8 oz) skinless pork chipolatas*

To make the batter, sift the flour and a pinch of salt into a large mixing bowl. Make a well in the middle, so that the bottom of the bowl is exposed. Break the eggs into this well and stir a little milk into them with a wooden spoon, delicately at first to avoid mixing in the flour, then gradually begin incorporating the flour, adding a little more milk as you go along. Go on stirring in the flour and adding small quantities of milk until the mixture is the consistency of cream. At this point you can beat the mixture thoroughly with an egg whisk. After a minute or two, if you wish, put the batter aside to stand for 1 hour.

Heat the butter or dripping in a baking tin, pour in the batter, drop the sausages in and bake in the oven at 220°C (425°F) mark 7 for 35 minutes. An unsophisticated vegetable should accompany this dish – boiled, buttered cabbage or sprouts.

N O T E : *It is important to have the baking tin and oven well heated. A warm tin, or cool oven, will stop the batter rising.*

If you have not experimented with batters before, you will be agreeably surprised by the transformation of the anaemic-looking raw batter into a billowing golden puff reminiscent of the best Yorkshire puddings.

Yorkshire Pudding

Almost everyone likes a good Yorkshire pudding, and it is easier to make than those flabby slices served up with institutional meals might lead you to expect. From the economy point of view, a generous helping of Yorkshire pudding will make people less greedy for roast beef.

4 SERVINGS

125 g (4 oz) plain flour	*300 ml (½ pint) milk*
a pinch of salt	*2 eggs*

Sift the flour and salt into a bowl, make a well in the centre and add the milk gradually, beating hard. Add the eggs, beating hard after each one. Put the batter into the fridge, or in a cool place, until 35 minutes before the roast has finished cooking. Pour half the fat from the roasting tin into another baking tin (or cake tin). Put the baking tin back into the oven until the fat is smoking hot, then pour in the batter. Cook the pudding at the top of the oven at 200°C (400°F) mark 6 for 30–35 minutes or until puffy and golden on top. (The roast has to be moved down to a lower shelf to finish cooking.)

Pancakes

Pancakes sprinkled with brown sugar and lemon juice, or filled with apricot jam, are an almost irresistible pudding. They are not difficult to make unless you are aiming for perfect circles, in which case you will need a cast-iron pan made specially for the purpose, straight-sided, like the ones used in Brittany, where pancakes are a local speciality. An ordinary medium-sized heavy-based frying pan gives less immaculate results, but the taste, after all, is the same.

Pancake batter is made like ordinary batter except that you add a little melted butter (see Toad-in-the-Hole, opposite, for instructions).

MAKES 8

125 g (4 oz) plain flour	*15-25 g (½-1 oz) butter, melted*
a pinch of salt	*1 egg and 1 egg yolk*
2 teaspoons caster sugar	*vegetable oil*
about 300 ml (½ pint) milk	

Sift the flour, salt and sugar into a bowl and proceed as for Toad-in-the-Hole until you have stirred in about half the milk and the batter is a thickish cream. Now stir in the butter and more milk until the batter is a *thin* cream. If you wish, leave it to stand in a cool place for an hour.

Heat the pan slowly until it is good and hot. With a pad of kitchen paper sprinkled with vegetable oil (you can use melted butter but oil is better because it doesn't burn and is tasteless) wipe a film of oil over the pan. The idea of greasing the pan is to prevent the batter sticking, *not* in any sense to fry the pancake. Drop a generous tablespoon of batter into the pan and immediately shake the pan gently with a clockwise turn of the wrist to spread the batter thinly over the bottom. Cook gently. As soon as the pancake edges can be easily detached, the pancake is ready to be turned over. Traditionally, you should toss it, which needs a strong wrist and an accurate eye. If tennis was not your strong suit, work a metal slice or spatula under the pancake and flip it over rapidly to brown the other side. As they are done, stack them on a plate in the oven, which should be warm, not hot.

N O T E : *For a change, you can try folding the whisked leftover egg white into your batter. This gives a fluffier-textured pancake. You can also vary the flavour of the batter itself by adding a little vanilla, grated lemon rind, or even a spoonful of brandy or rum if you happen to have such a thing. And the choice of fillings is enormous: apple purée, sultanas soaked in lemon juice and beaten into sweetened cream cheese, chopped walnuts and brown sugar, redcurrant jelly, to suggest only a few.*

Breton Buckwheat Pancakes

 Checking on my friends' current food preferences, one of them, Heather, explained that since her chef-son had married a Breton girl they had been eating a lot of buckwheat pancakes, now so popular with the family that they make them with a variety of fillings, sweet as well as savoury. Pancakes are ideal poor food in any case, wrapping up leftovers gracefully, or simply spread with jam or sprinkled with lemon juice and sugar. The buckwheat adds a nutty something, which is addictive. Try them.

MAKES 12 LARGE PANCAKES

250 g (9 oz) buckwheat flour	*2 eggs*
60 g (2½ oz) plain flour	*about 750 ml (1¼ pints) water and*
a pinch of salt	*milk, mixed in equal proportions*

Mix the dry ingredients together in a large bowl. Make a well in the centre and break in the eggs. Stir with a wooden spoon, gradually beating in the water and milk until you have a light batter. Leave to stand for 2 hours, if possible.

Grease a heavy-based frying pan with a piece of absorbent kitchen paper dipped in cooking oil. Heat the pan over a moderate heat and tip in a little batter, swirling it around in the pan to spread it in an even layer. After 1-2 minutes, by which time the underside should be lightly browned, flip the pancake over with a spatula, or toss it if you prefer! Cook for another 1-2 minutes. Remove the pan and keep warm while making the rest of the pancakes.

The pancakes can be filled immediately, for a gratin dish (see Note). Heather suggests cooked spinach with grated cheese; chopped ham and scrambled eggs; chopped ham or bacon with mushrooms. Or they can be prepared ahead, stacked with a piece of greaseproof paper between them to prevent sticking, and reheated by steaming over just bubbling water in a large pan. If you don't have a steamer, stand a plate on an inverted cup, in a large enough pan.

Suggested sweet fillings include: sultanas, honey and lemon; ice cream and maple syrup; soft fruits; home-made jam.

N O T E : *To make a dish of filled savoury pancakes more substantial, cover with a little cheesy béchamel sauce and a sprinkling of grated cheese, and heat through in the oven at 180°C (350°F) mark 4 for 20 minutes or so, flashing the top under the grill before serving to brown it.*

Breadcrumbs

Two sorts of breadcrumbs are extensively used in cooking – dried crumbs for coating food for frying (see Note), or sprinkling on top of various dishes cooked uncovered in the oven, and fresh crumbs for making various stuffings, dumpling mixtures, bread sauce, etc.

Dried crumbs are made by putting ends of loaves, crusts, leftover slices, etc., in a baking tin at the bottom of the oven to dry out while you are cooking other dishes. When they are dry, they are crushed. The easiest way is to wrap them in a cloth and to roll them with a rolling pin, then put them through a coarse sieve, and then store them in a screw-topped jar. They will keep for several weeks, if you remember to put the lid back at once after use. You *can* buy dry crumbs ready-made, but these look and taste odd, and the extra expense hardly seems justified when you can make your own easily and economically.

Fresh or soft breadcrumbs are made by rubbing white bread through a sieve or a grater or whizzing it briefly in a food processor. The bread should be a day old at least, and you should not use the crusts. If you are making a stuffing in a tremendous hurry, you can tear the bread up with your fingertips, but the result will be lumpier. Incidentally, fresh crumbs will not keep – they go mouldy in a trice – so you have to make them afresh each time.

N O T E : *In case you were wondering why foods are coated with crumbs, this is done for a reason, not merely for decoration. The breadcrumbs form a protective coating over the food which seals in the flavour and juices, and, in the case of fried food, is lighter and less greasy than batter.*

[10] Baked Polenta

8 SERVINGS

1.7 litres (3 pints) water	568 ml (1 pint) warm milk (or a
salt and pepper	mixture of milk and cream)
450 g (1 lb) coarsely ground	125 g (4 oz) Edam cheese, grated
cornmeal or polenta	freshly grated Parmesan or Pecorino
125 g (4 oz) butter	cheese
50 g (2 oz) plain flour	

Put the water in a large saucepan, add salt and bring to the boil. Reduce the heat and begin to pour in the cornmeal in a slow, steady stream, stirring all the time with a wooden spoon. When all the cornmeal has been added, simmer, stirring constantly, for 30 minutes or until the mixture starts to peel away from the sides of the pan.

Pour the polenta on to a clean surface (a wooden table or formica work top will do), and spread it until it is about 1 cm (½ inch) thick. It will begin to harden as it cools.

Melt half the butter in a large heavy-based saucepan and stir in the flour. Cook, stirring, for 2 minutes, then remove from the heat and gradually add the warm milk, stirring all the time. Bring to the boil, stirring, then simmer until the sauce is thick and smooth. Remove from the heat and stir in the grated Edam cheese until melted.

With a knife or pastry cutter, cut the polenta into small circles, and arrange these, slightly overlapping each other in layers in a shallow ovenproof dish or flan dish, dotting them here and there with fragments of the remaining butter. Pour over the cheese sauce, scatter the top with grated Parmesan and more fragments of butter and put in the oven at 200°C (400°F) mark 6 for about 20 minutes to heat up, bubble and go golden brown on the top.

[10] Pizza

Everybody loves pizza and really nothing could be easier or more economical. You don't have to use expensive mozzarella, olives, smoked sausages and anchovies. Pizza should be peasant food and some of the most successful combinations are not only less expensive but more original than classic pizzeria fare. The only English variant which would be a mistake, to my mind, is grated Cheddar. Your one really essential extravagance must be extra-virgin olive oil.

4-6 SERVINGS

700 g (1½ lb) strong white flour   *2 tablespoons olive oil*
1 teaspoon salt   *1 egg*
1 sachet fast action dried yeast   *warm water*

Combine the flour, salt and yeast in a large mixing bowl, pour in the oil and break in the egg. Make a well in the centre and begin to pour in the warm water, mixing all the time to make a dough. Go very gently with the water – as you knead the dough it will take in more flour than you expect. (If you do get it too wet, put it to rise in a very warm place and it should dry out a bit, before you knead it.)

Turn the dough on to a lightly floured surface and knead it for about 10 minutes or until it is smooth and elastic. (You can test this elasticity by pushing the dough ball with a finger; it should quickly spring back out to fill the identation.) Put the dough in a bowl, cover with a clean, damp cloth and leave it to rise in a warm place for about 1 hour.

When the dough has doubled in size, knock it back, knead it again, then pull or roll it out into two pizza bases. These can be any shape which will fit your baking sheets. Brush with oil and then put on your chosen topping (see below). Bake in the oven at 220°C (425°F) mark 7 for 15-20 minutes.

TOPPINGS:
• Stew some finely sliced onions very gently in olive oil. Spread these on the pizza base and sprinkle with salt and pepper.
• Tomato Sauce (see page 45), simply spread over the pizza base, makes *Pizza Rosso*.
• Dribble olive oil over the pizza base and sprinkle with salt to make *Pizza Bianca*, Rome's favourite mid-morning snack. A sprinkling of dried sage or rosemary is an optional addition.

● Fry tiny matchsticks of bacon in their own fat and scatter them over the pizza with some crumbled herby sausage and some chopped fresh marjoram or oregano (the traditional pizza herb). Break an egg on top and dribble with olive oil before baking.

VARIATION: **Calzone** is a pizza which has been wrapped around its filling, an Italian Cornish pasty. The filling can be southern, perhaps ricotta cheese and a couple of sun–dried tomatoes, or northern sausagemeat and finely shredded cabbage.

Fast Work

This is the chapter for evenings when you get back late from work, with two people expected for supper, or when a long car journey leaves everyone clamouring for immediate sustenance, or when you want a rapid but not skimpy meal after a late show – in fact for any of the occasions when a meal has to be prepared at the double, with materials to hand. Many of the recipes make use of canned foods, for convenience, but not too obviously – presumably no one needs advice on how to prepare baked beans on toast, and besides this is probably not what hungry people would consider a meal. Maximum preparation and cooking time is never more than an hour and, in most cases, considerably less. I have given the stages of preparation in some detail, to avoid fuss and fluster, and if you follow them carefully you should be able to produce a very presentable meal for two to four people – soup, main dish and even a pudding – in an hour, without becoming dishevelled, tired and irritable in the process.

This sort of cooking does require some forethought. You should keep a selection of tins to hand, as well as quite a few spices and herbs to ginger them up, and you will need the usual standbys – milk, eggs, butter, bread. For real emergencies, when the cupboard is practically bare, I have included one or two snack ideas.

Quick Onion Soup

The touch of inspiration in this recipe, given to me by a French friend, is the caramelising of the onions which gives the soup colour, body and a rich but delicate flavour all at once.

4 SERVINGS

25 g (1 oz) butter
4 large onions, thinly sliced
½ tablespoon sugar
1 litre (1¾ pints) hot water

1 vegetable stock cube
a dash of wine vinegar
salt and pepper (optional)

Melt the butter in a large frying pan and put in the onions. Stir them around until they begin to go soft, then put in the sugar. Keep stirring until the sugar browns – brown *not* black – and then pour in the hot water and stock cube with the vinegar. Simmer for 15 minutes, taste and add salt and pepper if necessary.
    Serve plain with buttered toast.

Chinese Egg Drop Soup

2 SERVINGS

125 g (4 oz) mushrooms, roughly
    chopped
a handful of watercress or spring
    onions, roughly chopped

600 ml (1 pint) Simple Stock (see
    page 21)
2 teaspoons soy sauce
1 egg

Simmer the mushrooms and cress or spring onions in the stock until tender. Add the soy sauce. Beat the egg and stir it rapidly through the bubbling soup until it forms yellow strands. Serve at once.

Chasse

I am including this recipe, originally a country-house breakfast dish, because it is an excellent way of combining the sort of odds and ends you can usually scrape together in the most depleted larder into a comforting little meal. The quantities I have given can be varied according to what is available – canned tomatoes can be used instead of fresh, or even a generous tablespoon of tomato purée, at a pinch.

2 SERVINGS

1 onion, chopped

a knob of butter

5 tomatoes, skinned and chopped

1 slice of cooked ham, or 2-3 rashers
    of bacon, de-rinded and chopped

3 cooked potatoes, diced

a dash of Worcestershire sauce

50-75 g (2-3 oz) Cheddar cheese,
    grated

a good pinch of paprika

2 eggs, poached

Fry the onion lightly in the butter, then add the tomatoes and ham or bacon. When these are hot, add the potatoes and a little water. Cook slowly for 5 minutes. Just before serving, add a dash of Worcestershire sauce and stir in the grated cheese and paprika. Serve with a poached egg on each helping.

Quick Welsh Rarebit

When you are in a tearing hurry, or faced with the job of concocting a meal out of a lump of stale cheese and some dry bread, Welsh Rarebit seems the obvious answer. The best cheese for this, I think, is Caerphilly, which gives a sharper, lighter texture than Cheddar, but I realise that this is a counsel of perfection.

2 SERVINGS

125-225 g (4-8 oz) cheese

1 teaspoon mustard powder

salt and pepper

a dash of Worcestershire sauce

1 egg, beaten

a knob of butter (optional)

2 slices of bread

Grate the cheese and mix it with the mustard, salt, pepper and Worcestershire sauce. Bind with the beaten egg. If you can spare it, a knob of butter worked in helps. Toast the bread on one side only. Spread the other side thickly with the mixture and stick it under the grill until the cheese topping is puffy and lightly browned. Eat at once.

VARIATIONS: Should you not have so much as an egg, you can thicken your cheese mixture (and make it go a bit further too) by stirring in a little cornflour, or flour, mixed with a little milk or water or beer. In that case you should really cook the Rarebit mixture in a saucepan for a few minutes to give the flour a chance to thicken. Then brown under the grill.

A couple of poached eggs on top, should you be well supplied with eggs, turns this into a Buck Rarebit.

Steamed Eggs

This is a handy way of cooking eggs, as a change from frying, baking or poaching them. For some reason, they taste better like this.

2 SERVINGS
a knob of butter   *salt and pepper*
2-4 eggs

Put a heatproof plate over a saucepan of boiling water (you could be cooking potatoes or a vegetable in the pan at the same time). Place a few scraps of butter on the plate. When they melt, crack the eggs carefully and slide them on to the plate. Sprinkle a little salt and pepper over them and cover with another inverted plate. Look at them after 3-4 minutes. They are ready when the whites are firm.

Tortilla

There is a knack to making a good tortilla, so that it emerges golden brown, compact and juicy without being undercooked. I once watched a chef in Seville cook tortillas, one after another, all perfect, and this is what he did. He used a small (20 cm/8 inch) well-seasoned cast-iron pan. In this he fried diced potato in olive oil until it was tender but not browned. In a bowl he rapidly whisked up some eggs with a pinch of coarse salt. He then tipped the potato into the egg mixture and let it sit while he wiped out the pan with more salt and kitchen paper. He put the pan back on the heat with a splash more olive oil, tipped the contents of the bowl into it all at once, gave the pan a quick shake and pressed the contents down with a metal slice, to compact them. After 2-3 minutes over a high flame he judged the tortilla was cooked underneath. With a practised flip of a muscular right arm, he tossed this substantial but small omelette into the air and caught it as it descended, cooked side uppermost. After a minute more over the heat the tortilla was ready to slide on to a plate and serve – and excellent eating it was too. I suggest you follow his method, using a non-stick pan, over lower heat and reversing the tortilla on to a plate before returning it to brown the base. If the potatoes, olive oil and eggs are all fresh and good quality, a tortilla needs nothing more. But you can pad out the basic mixture with various cooked leftovers – peas, chopped onions, cubes of chorizo, diced peppers, even pasta – to make it go further.

2 SERVINGS

2 biggish potatoes, weighing about	*4 eggs*
300 g (10 oz), peeled and diced	*200 ml (8 fl oz) olive oil*

Follow the method above, remembering that most of the olive oil is used to fry the diced potato, with a splash reserved for the tortilla.

 # Frittata Verde

Frittata, eggah, tortilla – basically these are the same thing spoken with different accents, a solid cake-like omelette where beaten eggs have been used to bind a tasty filling, usually cooked vegetables. I have suggested broad beans, peas and spring onions because these are usually to hand. A non-stick frying pan really comes into its own for the cooking.

4-6 SERVINGS

5 eggs	*1 bunch of spring onions, chopped*
1 small packet of frozen petits pois,	*salt and pepper*
thawed	*a little chopped parsley (optional)*
1 small packet of frozen broad beans,	*3 tablespoons olive oil*
thawed	

The broad beans need to be cooked for about 3 minutes. If you have time to slip the greyish skins off, well and good, if not don't worry, it will still taste good. The peas do not need cooking, but they should be completely thawed.

In a bowl, break the eggs, whisk lightly, then add all the vegetables, seasoning and parsley, if using. Heat the oil in the non-stick pan, then tip in all the eggy mixture at once, stir once or twice to distribute the vegetables, then turn the heat right down and cook for about 12-15 minutes, by which time the bottom should be solid and the top just runny. Lay a plate over the pan (wear rubber gloves), flip over so the frittata is on the plate, cooked side up, then slide it back into the pan for a few more minutes. You may find the flipping easier if you loosen the frittata from the pan first with a flexible spatula or slice. Lay the cooked frittata on a board on a sheet of kitchen paper, and cool if you can wait (it is more flavoursome at room temperature) or devour at once, with ratatouille or a salad.

VARIATION: Alternative filling suggestions: leftover pasta, grilled peppers, cooked mussels, cubed fried potatoes, leftover cooked broccoli.

Tunisian Salad

This makes a terrific accompaniment to grilled fish, like the red mullet often served with it in Tunisia. It's a colourful mélange of chopped raw vegetables, crisp but juicy, spiked with fresh chilli and seasoned with an elusive whiff of cumin. Serve with vinaigrette dressing to taste.

4 SERVINGS

1 cucumber, peeled, de-seeded and
   diced small
1 green pepper, de-seeded and
   chopped
450 g (1 lb) ripe tomatoes, skinned,
   de-seeded and chopped
1 bunch of spring onions, chopped
   with some of their green shoots

1 fresh green chilli, de-seeded and
   very finely chopped
½ teaspoon ground cumin
juice of ½ lemon
2 tablespoons olive oil
salt and pepper

Combine all the ingredients in a bowl, squeezing over the lemon juice. Add oil, salt and pepper, turn well and chill for about 30 minutes.

NOTE: *If you like chilli, you love it like this. If you find it too fiery, omit and instead add 1 tablespoon chopped fresh coriander.*

Potato, Apple and Caper Salad

4 SERVINGS

4 potatoes, scrubbed
2 small eating apples
3 celery sticks
1 tablespoon capers, drained

French Dressing (see page 169)
a squeeze of lemon juice
salt and pepper

Cook the potatoes in boiling water for about 20 minutes or until tender. Drain the potatoes, peel them and leave to cool.

Core and peel the apples. Slice the apples, potatoes and celery thinly and combine with the capers and dressing. Squeeze lemon juice over and season with salt and pepper.

This is good with most cold meat, particularly ham.

Poached Sausage and Hot Potato Salad

A hot potato salad, if you have never tried it, combines very pleasantly with those smoked sausage rings stocked by most supermarkets and delicatessens.

2-3 SERVINGS

2 large potatoes, scrubbed	*salt and black pepper*
1 smoked sausage	*1 tablespoon finely chopped onion*
1 teaspoon mustard powder, or	*a little chopped fresh parsley*
2 teaspoons French mustard	*(optional)*
4 tablespoons oily French Dressing	*pickled onions or gherkins, to serve*
(see page 169)	

Bring two pans of water to the boil. Put the potatoes in one and the sausage ring in the other. The sausage should simmer, not boil, for 5–10 minutes until hot. I think the flavour is improved by removing the polythene wrap, never mind what the makers tell you.

After about 20 minutes, test the potatoes with a fork. When they are tender, take them out and peel them, holding them in a cloth. Cut them into smallish chunks. Stir the mustard into the vinaigrette dressing and pour over the potatoes, spooning them about gently to spread the dressing evenly. Sprinkle with salt and black pepper. Add the chopped onion and parsley, if using, and spoon around a bit more.

Take the sausage out of its cooking water, cut it into chunks and serve with a few pickled gherkins or onions, which go well with this dish, and the salad.

Salmon Soufflé

Making a soufflé is not at all difficult as long as you do it methodically, stage by stage. If you deviate from the routine you are apt to get flustered and this will spoil your appetite, if not the soufflé.

2-3 SERVINGS

1 small can of salmon	*2 teaspoons plain flour*
4 eggs	*150 ml (¼ pint) milk*
butter for greasing	*a pinch of salt*
FOR THE WHITE SAUCE	*1 teaspoon paprika*
25 g (1 oz) butter	

Drain the can of salmon, reserving the liquid. Pick out any bones or skin and mash the salmon with a fork. Take two mixing bowls, one large, one smaller, and carefully break *three* egg yolks into the larger bowl and *four* whites into the smaller one. Whisk the white until firm but not too dry.

Make the white sauce base for the soufflé. Melt the butter in a saucepan, stir in the flour and cook for 1-2 minutes, stirring. Remove from the heat and gradually stir in the milk. Bring to the boil, stirring constantly, then simmer over a low heat until smooth and thick. Add the salmon liquid, salt and paprika and stir together. Stir in the mashed salmon, heating until warmed through.

Grease a 900 ml (1½ pint) soufflé dish with a little butter. Beat the egg yolks and stir in the salmon mixture thoroughly. Into this, you now fold the beaten egg whites, using a circular action. The idea is to distribute the egg white throughout the heavier salmon base, but not to labour the point to the extent of driving out all the air bubbles.

Turn the whole lot into the prepared dish and bake in the oven at 200°C (400°F) mark 6 for 20-25 minutes or until the soufflé is well risen and the top is firm and slightly browned. A few peas are all you need with this.

V A R I A T I O N : Canned tuna fish makes a more substantial soufflé.

 ## Grilled Herring or Mackerel with Mustard

1 SERVING

1 herring or mackerel	*a little butter*
English or French mustard	*a squeeze of lemon juice (optional)*

Have the fish cleaned and opened out flat like a kipper. Smear both sides fairly generously with mustard. Put a little butter in the grill pan, after removing the rack. Heat gently and, when it begins to sizzle, put the fish in, skin side up. Immediately turn the fish over and continue cooking for about 5 minutes. It will not need to be turned again.

A squeeze of lemon juice heightens the flavour. Plain boiled potatoes are the best accompaniment to highly seasoned fish dishes.

Fish Baked in a Salt Crust

I doubt there can be a more delicious way to bake a fish, or a simpler one. The salt forms a protective crust under which the fish sweetly cooks, emerging tender, its flavour subtly 'de-fished' as the Chinese put it. The flavour is not salty (though you must take care over the unveiling process) but sweetish, as fresh fish are. And the skin peels off like a glove. I often use this method to cook a small bream, for two, and use a whole carton of table salt. Properly, the salt should be that greyish substance called *gros sel* in France; it is cheap there, less so here. Try the table salt version, and if it appeals, do a bigger fish for a dinner party, which you treat to a *gros sel* crust.

2 SERVINGS

1 small whole bream, gutted but with the head on, weighing about 700 g (1½ lb)	*1 carton of table salt*

The more neatly the dish fits the fish the further your salt will go. If you don't have an oval ovenproof dish, improvise an oval container of foil inside a standard baking tin. Cover the bottom generously with salt, lay the fish on top, then cover with the remaining salt. It does not need to be inches thick, but no fish should be visible. Bake in the oven at 190°C (375°F) mark 5 for 30 minutes, then leave to cool for a moment. Gingerly, scrape off the top crust. You will find the skin comes away easily. Now push back the loose salt around it to prevent it going on to the fish itself. Carefully remove the top half with a slice. Lift off the spine and bones, and gently extract the other half. Place on warmed plates and serve with melted butter to which you add a squeeze of lemon juice and a tiny sprinkling of cayenne, and boiled new potatoes.

N O T E : *With gros sel the salt forms a compacted crust, much less fiddly to handle as you can crack it with a flourish to reveal your festive fish, maybe a larger bream, a small bass, even a sea trout.*

A Meal in a Potato

Large baked potatoes with a little something tucked inside are a godsend when you are hard pressed, or hard up. All you need is one or two (depending on how hungry you feel) large potatoes per person, some grated cheese, butter, salt and pepper. And, if you want to make a pretty solid meal of it, an egg for each potato.

1 SERVING

1-2 large potatoes, scrubbed	*about 50 g (2 oz) cheese, grated*
salt and pepper	*freshly grated nutmeg (optional)*
a knob of butter	*1 egg (optional)*

Dry the potatoes and rub salt into the skins. Bake in the oven at 220°C (425°F) mark 7 for about 1 hour or until they feel soft when pinched. Cut a cap off each potato and scoop out a little pulp. Put a knob of butter and a handful of grated cheese in the hollow, and sprinkle with salt and pepper. A little nutmeg is nice too. Return to the oven for a few minutes. If you want an egg too, scoop out rather more of the potato pulp, proceed as before except that you break an egg in before putting back the cap. Cook for 7 minutes or until the egg is set.

VARIATION: Another variation on this meal-in-a-potato theme is kidneys baked in potatoes. It takes longer but is very appetising, if you like kidneys. Scrub and bake the potatoes for 1 hour as above. Cut a slice off the top and scoop out some of the inside. Skin the kidneys and rub in salt, pepper and a little mustard. Roll each kidney in a rasher of bacon and put in a potato case. Wrap the potatoes in foil with a scrap of butter and bake for 1 hour longer. The kidney gravy is soaked up by the potato.

Potato Latkes

This is a Jewish dish, and a very tasty one, substantial enough to serve on its own with some slices of garlic sausage and a plate of pickled gherkins. Latkes, definitely not recommended for calorie counters, are made of grated raw potato and onion, bound with egg and flour, and fried until brown on both sides.

4–6 SERVINGS

450 g (1 lb) potatoes	2 large (size 1) eggs, beaten
1 tablespoon grated or finely chopped onion	salt and black pepper
	vegetable oil for frying
2 tablespoons plain flour	

Peel and grate the potatoes into a mixing bowl. Add the onion and flour, then stir in the eggs and season with salt and pepper. The mixture should be soft enough to drop from a spoon. If it seems too dry or stiff, add another egg.

Heat some oil in a frying pan and, when it is hot, drop in spoonfuls of the mixture and fry until brown on both sides, turning the potato cakes with a spatula. Serve at once.

Chicken Parcels with Lemon and Sesame

This is a top favourite dish with my teenage daughter and her friends. I think they are seduced by the idea of tantalisingly aromatic food to un-wrap on the plate. The Japanese seasonings do a lot for supermarket chicken pieces, skinned and trimmed, but for special treats I usually make it with chicken breasts only. It usually pays to buy two or three small chickens rather than pieces because the bones and trimmings make an invaluable stock (see page 21).

4-6 SERVINGS

3 tablespoons white sesame seeds
1 teaspoon black peppercorns
1 small bunch of spring onions, finely chopped, including some green tops
150 ml (¼ pint) light soy sauce

1 tablespoon light brown sugar
4-6 chicken breasts, skinned and cut into bite-sized pieces
1 large lemon, sliced
1 tablespoon peanut (groundnut) oil
a few drops of sesame oil (optional)

Place the sesame seeds and peppercorns in a dry pan and shake over heat until the seeds jump and smell toasty. Crush both in a mortar. Mix the crushed spice, onion, soy sauce and sugar in a bowl. Add the chicken, turn well to coat and leave for about 1 hour to absorb the fla-vours.

Cut four pieces of foil about 15 cm (6 inches) square, oil them, then spoon a heap of chicken with some marinade on to each square. Lay a thin slice of lemon on top, sprinkle with a little lemon juice, then wrap neatly and bake on a baking sheet in the oven at 190°C (375°F) mark 5 for 30 minutes or until well cooked but tender.

Serve with a small pile of Chinese egg noodles, sprinkled with soy and sesame oil, and a big green salad.

 ## Hash

2 SERVINGS

2 onions, roughly chopped
butter for frying
2-3 boiled potatoes, diced
some boiled cabbage or Brussels sprouts, chopped

1 small can of corned beef
salt and pepper

Fry the onions in a little butter until soft. Add the potatoes and cabbage or sprouts, and fry gently until they are warmed through. Cut the corned beef into chunks and add to the frying pan. Cook over a moderate heat, stirring from time to time, until the corned beef has mingled with the other ingredients into a sort of mush. Use a little more butter if the mixture looks dry and in danger of sticking to the pan. Add lots of pepper and a little salt if needed, though corned beef is salty enough, so don't overdo it. You can, if you like, break a couple of eggs on top of the hash, at this point, and cover the pan until they are set.

If you feel the need for extra vegetables, I suggest boiled or steamed carrots.

 ## Liver au Poivre

Everyone knows steak au poivre, where the raw meat is coated in crushed peppercorns before grilling or frying. Liver au poivre is my own variant and is both very good and very cheap as meat dishes go these days. Use pig's liver, which is cheaper than lamb's. The secret of palatable liver is not to overcook it. The quick-fry method here, plus the coating of peppercorns, keeps the liver tender and gives it an excellent flavour.

2-3 SERVINGS

225 g (8 oz) pig's liver　　　　　　*2 tablespoons vegetable oil*
2 teaspoons black peppercorns

With a sharp knife, slice the liver into narrow strips about 5 mm (¼ inch) thick. Crush the peppercorns to a gritty consistency in a grinder, or pestle and mortar, or, failing that, by folding them in a tea towel and banging them with a blunt instrument. Sprinkle over the sliced liver until well coated. Heat the oil in a frying pan, drop in the sliced liver and fry over a high heat for about 3 minutes, turning with a spoon until lightly browned on all sides. As soon as the liver pieces have stiffened, without being hard, they are done.

Good with chips and a green salad.

Soufflé Omelette

A nice, quick pudding, which you can fill with whatever is available – apricot jam, apple purée, even marmalade.

2 SERVINGS

3 eggs, separated
2 tablespoons double cream
  (optional)
1 tablespoon caster sugar

50 g (2 oz) butter
apricot jam, apple purée or
  marmalade, to fill
icing sugar, to dust

Beat the egg yolks, cream (if using) and sugar together until smooth. Whisk the egg whites until stiff and fold lightly into the yolks. Melt the butter in a frying pan over a moderate heat, pour in the egg mixture, level it off with a spoon and leave until small bubbles appear on the top. Spoon in the jam or whatever filling you are using, fold the omelette over and dust the top with icing sugar. Serve at once.

Baked Bananas

I think this is the nicest way of eating bananas. It is also very quick and easy to prepare.

2 SERVINGS

4 large bananas
1 tablespoon brown sugar
juice of 1 orange

juice of ½ lemon
a little grated orange and lemon rind
butter

Peel the bananas and slice in half lengthways. Arrange them in a shallow ovenproof dish. Sprinkle with brown sugar and pour over the orange and lemon juice. Sprinkle with a little grated orange and lemon rind. Dot fairly liberally with butter and bake, uncovered, in the oven at 180°C (350°F) mark 4 for about 20 minutes or until the bananas are soft and the other ingredients have turned to a thin syrup.

Serve exactly as they are – cream would be too cloying.

VARIATIONS: A few sultanas sprinkled over the dish is a pleasant addition. And, if you have any rum around the place, a spoonful added with the other ingredients gives you Baked Bananas Creole.

Poor Knights

This is a recipe for using up stale bread.

3 tablespoons brown sugar
150 ml (¼ pint) milk
slices of stale bread about 1 cm (½
  inch) thick

2 egg yolks, beaten
oil and/or butter for shallow frying
about ½ teaspoon ground cinnamon
brown sugar, to sprinkle

Stir the sugar into the milk. Cut the bread into soldiers and put them in the milk and sugar for a few moments on each side, turning them over carefully. (Do not over-handle them or they will become soggy.) Dip each one into the beaten egg and then fry in hot oil or butter until golden and crispy. Serve sprinkled with the cinnamon and more brown sugar.

Caramel Oranges

This is a simple fruit salad of sliced oranges glorified by a sprinkling of crushed caramel, like amber chips. Use a sharp knife to prepare the oranges and take off every scrap of outer pith, which sticks in one's teeth and spoils the taste. Hold the oranges over the dish you are serving them in while preparing them so none of the juice is wasted.

2 SERVINGS
3 oranges
juice of 1 orange

4 tablespoons sugar

Slice the peel off the oranges, downwards rather than round and round, and trim off every bit of pith. Slice the oranges thickly, picking out the pips. Put the orange slices in a bowl with the orange juice and 1 tablespoon sugar. Alternatively, if you have time, boil up a little sugar, water and orange juice and pour it on the oranges when cooled.

To make the caramel, heat the remaining sugar in an enamelled pan with a little water, until it melts and goes brown – golden brown, not treacle coloured. Pour on to a sheet of greased paper to cool. When it is hard and brittle, shatter it by hitting it with something heavy, such as a bottle or rolling pin. Scatter the fragments over the fruit salad.

Pasta Faster

The most obvious candidate for a chapter all to itself in a paupers' cookbook of the 1990s, is pasta, that staple food of Italy and South-East Asia which is rapidly becoming the world's favourite cheap and cheerful fast food. I know scarcely anyone who does not eat some form of pasta dish two or three times a week, and students, in particular, seem to eat pasta almost every day. The reasons are obvious: pasta is cheap, filling and endlessly versatile, and it enables hungry people to be fed in 15 minutes flat. Not that all the recipes in this section are of that order; it is also possible, and desirable, to extend your repertoire to include some of the more elaborate and time-consuming pasta-based dishes, such as the variations on lasagne, the odd timballo, even home-made ravioli with various fillings, all of which have enough clout to form the main dish at a dinner party.

My own discovery where pasta is concerned is more of a rediscovery. After some years of preferring the so-called 'fresh' pasta on supermarket shelves, I have been reconverted by Italian cookery writers, like Marcella Hazan and Anna del Conte, to the superior merits of the dried variety, now available in a profusion of different shapes and sizes in any supermarket which knows its business. Fresh pasta is brilliant if you buy it from a reputable Italian grocer, or delicatessen, or

97

if you make it yourself (a skill I recommend any serious pasta fan to acquire). You can make your own fresh pasta from nothing more than strong white flour and an egg or two, so it makes good 'emergency' food, and you might prefer to serve fresh pasta on special occasions, when you have reason to suppose that your guests will appreciate the extra lightness and subtle texture of the real hand-made article. However, for everyday, a good-quality dried pasta made from durum wheat (as most of them are), is infinitely preferable to the standard 'fresh' pasta commonly available. When cooked correctly, dried pasta has the ideal 'springy' texture and a mild but inimitable flavour all its own. By comparison, most bought fresh pasta is flaccid, sticky with starch, and characterless. And it costs more. The explanation, according to the experts, is that this type of pasta is not made from the correct durum wheat flour, and so does not provide that slight bouncy chewiness that distinguishes the authentic pasta cooked *al dente* – in fact the term *al dente* is rendered almost meaningless in this context.

Another small but significant discovery I have made is that pasta should not be drained too rigorously. Italians tip out most of the cooking water, but not the last drop. A couple of tablespoons left in the pan helps prevent the pasta coagulating into a sticky lump while you are completing the sauce, seasonings and other additions. Nor, when using dried pasta, is there any need to rinse off extra starch, as there is with the 'fresh' type. Once the dried pasta is cooked *al dente*, tip off most but not all the cooking water, splash a little olive oil into the pan, give it a good shake and you can leave it in a warm place safely for up to 5 minutes, while you get on with the other preparations. It also makes an important difference if your serving dish (a big round bowl or platter is a lot more simpatico than a saucepan for presenting pasta) and plates are all piping hot. A pair of wooden forks is ideal for tossing and mixing pasta and additions, plus a large spoon for serving.

A good fruity olive oil represents real added value when used for tossing cooked pasta; a couple of spoonfuls makes it glisten appetisingly, and creates a splendid aromatic 'nose'. Keep the lesser oils for frying the sauce ingredients if you need to cut back. Ready-grated Parmesan cheese, though handy, is about as tasteless as tea-bag tea, and pricy to boot. Often, too, it is unnecessary. There are many bone-simple pasta recipes, as you can see from those in this chapter, where the cheese treatment is out of place, and these are increasingly the ones I prefer; a lot of pasta is lightly coated with a little pungent seasoning and dished up hot, shiny and fragrant. True Southern food, at once stimulating and soothing.

Finally, for the worriers among you, a word of reassurance about timing. Well, maybe it's not so reassuring, if you are the scatty type of cook. The truth is that pasta, both dried and fresh, needs watching and testing while it cooks, to determine 'doneness'. Whatever the packet instructions say, you would be wise to start checking sooner than the time given; the simplest foodstuffs need a little care to give of their best. Fork out a strand or morsel and chew it. If the centre is still chalky, uncooked, give it a minute or two longer. When it is almost tender right through but just chewy is right for any dish that will be cooked a moment or two longer, while tossing with sauces and seasonings. If, for some reason, the pasta will need to be kept warm in the oven, it can do with being slightly undercooked. If you are going to dump it straight on to hot plates, with a spoonful of sauce to be added individually, the pasta can be cooked a little longer until it is more tender, only faintly resistant.

Making Fresh Pasta

Having sifted 550 g (1¼ lb) flour and a pinch of salt on to a floured work surface, make a well in the centre and break into it 5 large eggs or, for pasta *verde* (green pasta), 4 eggs and 75 g (3 oz) of puréed cooked spinach. Using two fingers, draw the flour into the egg mix until it lumps together.

Slap the lump down and attack with the heels of both hands with a scrubbing action which stretches the dough away from you. Gather up and repeat the process for not less than 15 minutes. Then divide the dough into lumps.

Flatten each lump by rolling vigorously with a floury rolling pin, from the middle outwards in all directions. At first it will spring back but suddenly it will grow thinner, wider. Roll it thinly then lay it on a cloth over the back of a chair.

A pasta machine can save you this last step. Pass the dough through the mangle and it will stretch it finely, though not to any great width. To make pasta ribbons – or tagliatelle – set the machine with grooved rollers to slice to the width you want: 0.5 cm (¼ inch) gives slim noodles.

Pasta comes in all shapes and sizes. For ravioli, roll out a rectangle of fresh pasta. Divide one half into lightly marked squares and spoon meat filling into the centre of each square. Moisten the other half of the pasta, fold over the meat-filled squares, press down firmly with your hand and lightly edge with a pastry cutter.

Spaghetti with Lemon

If possible, use the richer and more expensive egg pasta, *al uovo*, for this dish.

6 SERVINGS

salt

grated rind of 2 lemons and juice of
   1 large lemon

175 g (6 oz) crème fraîche, or
   whipped or double cream

1 teaspoon freshly grated nutmeg

1 teaspoon black pepper

450 g (1 lb) spaghetti or spaghettini

freshly grated Parmesan cheese, to
   serve

Fill a large saucepan with slightly salted water and bring to the boil. Put the lemon rind and juice into the dish in which you'll serve the spaghetti. Add the crème fraîche or cream, nutmeg and pepper.

Cook the spaghetti in the boiling water for about 8 minutes or until just tender. Drain, and toss in the lemon mixture. Serve with plenty of freshly grated Parmesan cheese.

Spaghetti all'Arrabbiata

The 'raging' of the title refers to the 'blaze' imparted by dried chillies. This is not for the tender palate, but a fine, appetising and fast way to serve spaghetti for those who like it hot.

4 SERVINGS

3-4 dried red chillies

3-4 garlic cloves, chopped

½ × 50 g (2 oz) can of anchovies,
   mashed

450 g (1 lb) spaghetti

6 tablespoons olive oil

salt and pepper

Prepare the red chillies as described on page 119, and pound them roughly in a pestle and mortar with the garlic and anchovies. Put this mixture in a wide flameproof dish and stand it on an asbestos mat over a very low heat. Cook the pasta in boiling salted water for about 8 minutes or until just tender. The spaghetti should look creamy pale, and be flexible but not sticky. Drain, reserving 1 tablespoon of the cooking water. Combine the spaghetti with the other ingredients in the hot dish, adding the reserved cooking water and the oil. Season and toss well with forks, then serve immediately on hot plates.

N O T E : *The quantity of chillies is approximate. Nervous types can begin with one or two, removing the seeds, where most of the 'hotness' lies. I remove the seeds from one or two, myself, leaving them in the other chillies.*

Spaghetti with Red Clam Sauce

This recipe is just as good with mussels and other shellfish.

4 SERVINGS

450 g (1 lb) clams
350 g (12 oz) spaghetti (preferably egg, al uovo, spaghetti)
salt and black pepper
4 tablespoons olive oil
3 garlic cloves, crushed

a glass of white wine
1½ tablespoons tomato purée
a pinch of sugar (optional)
a bunch of fresh parsley, finely chopped

Wash the clams carefully and make sure they are all fighting to stay shut when you tap them. Any that gape must be thrown away.

Cook the pasta in plenty of boiling salted water for about 8 minutes or until just tender. Meanwhile, heat the olive oil in a heavy-based saucepan large enough to hold the drained spaghetti, add the garlic and cook until it is just beginning to take on some colour; do not let it burn. Pour in the wine and let it bubble for a couple of minutes, then stir in the tomato purée and cook for 1 minute. Season with black pepper, the sugar, if using, and a little salt. (Don't overdo the salt as there is plenty occurring naturally in the clams and the tomato purée.) Add the clams and turn them in the hot oil and wine. The moment all the clams have opened, remove the pan from the heat and stir in the parsley. Drain the spaghetti and stir it into the clams and their sauce. Serve at once on warmed plates.

Orechiette with Peas and Mint

 A wonderful way to use the first peas – so delicate it's better without Parmesan.

6 SERVINGS

salt
900 g (2 lb) fresh new peas
125 g (4 oz) butter
2 shallots or 1 small onion, finely chopped

450 g (1 lb) orechiette
a bunch of fresh mint, torn into small pieces

Fill a large saucepan with plenty of salted water and put it on a high heat. Shell the peas and blanch them for about 1 minute in boiling water in a separate saucepan. Strain the peas but keep the water.

Heat the butter in a heavy-based saucepan, add the shallots or onion and cook gently until softened but not browned. Put the orechiette in the boiling water and cook for about 8 minutes or until almost tender. Put the peas in with the shallots over a low heat. Add the mint, a pinch of salt and 1-2 tablespoons of the pea liquor. Drain the pasta and serve with the sauce on top.

Pasta Shells with Prawns

Shellfish stalls sell their prawns in pints. From a supermarket, about 225 g (8 oz) prawns will do, but they must be in their shells as the stock made from these gives this dish its flavour. Parmesan should not be served with fish sauces.

6 SERVINGS

sunflower or olive oil
600 ml (1 pint) cooked prawns in their shells
250 ml (8 fl oz) white wine
250 ml (8 fl oz) water
350 g (12 oz) pasta shells

salt and black pepper
2 garlic cloves, crushed
150 ml (¼ pint) single cream
a pinch of freshly grated nutmeg
a bunch of fresh parsley, finely chopped

Heat 2 teaspoons sunflower or olive oil in a small, heavy-based saucepan. Remove the prawns from their shells and put the shells and heads in the hot oil. Turn the shells round in the oil until they stop sizzling loudly, then pour over the glass of wine. Let it evaporate for a moment, then add the glass of water. Cover and simmer for at least 30 minutes to extract maximum flavour from the shells. Strain the stock through a sieve, then return it to the pan and continue to simmer until the stock has reduced to about 100-175 ml (4-6 fl oz).

Cook the pasta in plenty of boiling salted water for about 8 minutes or until just tender. Meanwhile, put the garlic in a heavy pan deep enough to hold all the pasta, and heat gently until it is just translucent, then turn up the heat and add the peeled prawns. Drain the pasta and stir it in with the prawns, then pour over the condensed prawn stock and the cream. Season with lots of black pepper and nutmeg. Stir in the parsley and serve immediately on hot plates.

Japanese Cold Noodles

The advantage of these cold noodles is that they can be prepared and left in the fridge or larder for a day and a night, if it is more convenient to cook them in advance.

4-5 SERVINGS

500 ml (18 fl oz) dashi or chicken stock
200 ml (7 fl oz) dry sherry
200 ml (7 fl oz) dark soy sauce
5 cm (2 inch) piece of fresh root ginger, peeled and grated

6 spring onions, finely sliced (including green parts)
450 g (1 lb) dried Japanese or Italian noodles

Put the dashi or stock, sherry and soy sauce in a saucepan, bring to the boil, then remove from the heat and leave to cool.

Stir the ginger and onions into the cooled sauce. Cook the noodles in boiling water following packet instructions or until cooked but still firm. Drain, then rinse under cold running water and drain again. Transfer to a serving dish and pour over the sauce. Serve at once, or cover and store in the fridge until required.

Pasta and Chickpea Salad

This is one of the best store-cupboard salads, the bland, tender pasta and firm, nutty chickpeas adding up to one of those truly irresistible pairings of texture and taste. Eat this alone, or with crisp green salad leaves, or as an accompaniment to cold meat, or hot grilled sausages or chops. I find this dish so useful and more-ish that I try to make a big bowlful every week, using up most of the chickpeas prepared as described on page 67.

6-8 SERVINGS

225 g (8 oz) chickpeas, soaked overnight
450 g (1 lb) penne, farfelle or conchiglie
salt and pepper
1 bunch of spring onions, chopped

about 250 ml (8 fl oz) well seasoned vinaigrette, made with some garlic and a dash of fresh lemon juice (see page 169)
a small handful of fresh parsley or coriander, chopped

103

Drain the chickpeas and put them in a large saucepan. Cover with fresh water, bring to the boil and cook for 2-3 hours (depending on the age of the chickpeas) or until they are nutty but tender. Drain well.

Meanwhile, cook the pasta in boiling salted water for about 8 minutes or until just tender. Drain and put in a big dish with the chickpeas. Add the spring onions and vinaigrette slowly, tasting and tossing while the ingredients are still hot, until you have added just enough. Add the parsley or coriander, salt and pepper, and a squeeze more lemon juice if you like. It should all glisten attractively. Serve at room temperature, not chilled.

Pasta with Broccoli and Anchovies

My daughter, Daisy, introduced me to this excellent pasta dish which has a Sicilian lustiness of flavour. If you faithfully follow the instructions, it is foolproof, and can be served as a main dish after a starter of grilled red peppers. A wide, but not too shallow, heatproof pottery bowl that can go into the oven safely, or stand on a hotplate over a heat diffuser, makes the final assembly of this (and many other pasta dishes) easier.

4-6 SERVINGS

2 heads of firm green broccoli (about 350 g/12 oz)
salt and pepper
1½ × 500 g (1 lb) packet of penne or farfalle

50 g (2 oz) can of anchovies, drained
4 garlic cloves, chopped
1 dried red chilli (optional)
4-6 tablespoons fruity olive oil

Remove any woody ends and yellowing leaves from the broccoli. Cut the stems off and chop them into chunks. Cook the stems and florets as described on page 111, then drain, reserving the cooking water. Chop the cooked broccoli to a coarse mush.

Meanwhile, bring a large saucepan of salted water to the boil, add the pasta and cook for about 8 minutes. Pound the anchovies, garlic and chilli, if you want that fiery tingle, to a pulp in a mortar with a pestle or in a strong bowl with the end of a rolling pin. Put a shallow, flameproof dish on an asbestos mat over a very low heat and add the olive oil. When it is hot, add the anchovy mixture, stir and bubble for 1 minute, then add the chopped broccoli, mixing with forks. Let it all get thoroughly hot.

By now, the pasta should be *al dente*, tender but still chewy in the middle. Drain quickly and tip the pasta into the flameproof dish. Toss

104

thoroughly, adding a little of the reserved broccoli water if it seems too dry. Heat through for 1 minute, then serve on hot plates.

 ## Pasta with Peas, Cream, Bacon and Thyme

Made with canned *piselli* (petits pois) and pancetta, this will taste more authentic and Italian. However, an Anglicised version using frozen petits pois and diced smoked bacon or gammon, is also excellent. I once ate this with pasta authority Lizzie Spender, and she added a couple of spoonfuls of vodka, which gave it a certain *frisson*, but this is optional.

6-8 SERVINGS

1½ × 500 g (1 lb) packet of penne, farfalle or conchiglie
salt and pepper
3 tablespoons olive oil or 50 g (2 oz) butter
2 onions, chopped
2 garlic cloves, crushed
100-150 g (4-5 oz) pancetta, chopped, or bacon, de-rinded and diced

2 cans of petits pois, drained, or 2 × 500 g (1 lb) packet of frozen petits pois
several sprigs of fresh thyme
150 ml (5 fl oz) carton of single cream

Cook the pasta in plenty of boiling salted water for 8 minutes or until just tender. Meanwhile, heat the oil or butter in a saucepan, add the onion and garlic, cover and cook over a low heat until softened. Add the pancetta or bacon and cook until opaque but not brown. Add the canned or frozen peas, cover and heat through. Pinch the thyme leaves from the stalks and add them to the peas.

Drain the pasta and tip it into a warmed serving dish. Add the cream to the peas, bubble up quickly, season with salt and pepper and toss with the pasta. Serve on hot plates.

 ## Pasta with Borlotti Beans

Canned borlotti beans, like canned chickpeas, are a useful store-cupboard standby. They look attractive, with their pink marbled skins, and this is an Italian way to serve them, contrasting with plain cooked pasta. The dish is halfway between a soup and a pasta dish.

6-8 SERVINGS

3 tablespoons olive oil

1 large onion, chopped

2 large carrots, diced

2 celery sticks, sliced

75 g (3 oz) pancetta, smoked bacon
   or gammon, diced

2 × 432 g (15 oz) can of borlotti
   beans

salt and pepper

450 g (1 lb) conchiglie or farfalle

chopped fresh rosemary

freshly grated Parmesan cheese, to
   serve (optional)

Heat the oil in a heavy-based saucepan, add the onion, carrot and celery, stir and fry over a low heat until soft. Add the diced pancetta,
gammon or bacon, and continue cooking until thoroughly amalga-
mated and quite dark. Stir in the borlotti beans with some of their
liquid, season with salt and pepper, and leave to heat through.

Meanwhile, cook the pasta in plenty of boiling water for about 8
minutes or until just tender. Drain quickly and add to the pan. Mix
well and add more bean liquid if the mixture seems too dry. Stir in a
generous amount of chopped fresh rosemary and serve. Some fresh
Parmesan can be dusted over this dish, for richness.

VARIATION: Add a can of tomatoes to the softened vegetables
for colour and body.

Pasta with Leeks and Mussels

You could replace the butter in this recipe with olive oil – which would
be better for your heart – but the leeks won't caramelise in the same
way, and it is the sweetness of the leeks which makes this dish. If you
like the sweet flavour, you can turn this into more of a party dish by
adding one or two fresh dates. Stone them, slice them lengthways into
strips, and put them in when you fry the leeks.

6-8 SERVINGS

450 g (1 lb) mussels

1½ × 500 g (1 lb) packet of penne
   or farfalle

salt

75 g (3 oz) butter

450 g (1 lb) leeks, cut into 1 cm
   (½ inch) slices

Scrub the mussels clean, removing all the barnacles and hairy bits and
discarding any which don't shut when tapped on the side of the sink.

Cook the pasta in plenty of boiling salted water for about 8 minutes,

106

or until just tender. Meanwhile, heat the butter in a sauté pan or heavy-based saucepan deep enough to hold all the mussels, add the leeks and cook them until they begin to caramelise without becoming too soft. Add the mussels, cover with a lid and cook for 20 seconds. Remove the lid and lift out the mussels one by one as they open. Wearing rubber gloves, shell the mussels over the pan, so that none of the juice is lost, and remove the flesh to a warm plate. Leave some of the mussels in their shells or half-shells to make the dish more attractive. Drain the pasta and pour over the mussels, leeks and buttery juices. Serve at once on warmed plates.

Pasta with Courgettes and Cream

A light summery dish. I suggest penne as the pasta shape, as they echo the courgette sticks in size.

6 SERVINGS

6 small courgettes
salt and pepper
4 tablespoons olive oil
2 garlic cloves, finely chopped
500 g (1 lb) packet of penne

150 ml (5 fl oz) carton of double
  cream
fresh mint or basil leaves, torn into
  small pieces

Slice the courgettes lengthways, remove some seeds, then slice again lengthways into quarters, then into little sticks. Place these in a colander, sprinkle lightly with salt and leave to sweat for 10-15 minutes to extract some moisture.

Heat the oil in a frying pan or in a large flameproof pottery dish, and add the garlic. Fry for 1 minute, then add the courgette pieces and cook for about 10 minutes or until tender, turning to prevent them catching and burning, and reducing the heat if necessary.

Meanwhile, cook the penne in plenty of boiling salted water for about 8 minutes, or until just tender. Add the cream to the courgettes, bring to the boil, stirring, then add the torn herb leaves. Drain the pasta, stir it into the courgettes and serve at once on hot plates.

Fettucine with Smoked Salmon

Smoked salmon pieces, or scraps, turn up in delicatessens and on market stalls cheaply enough to make this a pauper's pasta, especially as a little goes a long way, flavour-wise.

4 SERVINGS

275 g (10 oz) fettucine
salt and black pepper
1 tablespoon olive oil
15 g (½ oz) butter
a small bunch of spring onions, finely
    chopped
125-175 g (4-6 oz) smoked salmon
    scraps, trimmed into neat shreds,
    dark bits removed

150 ml (5 fl oz) carton of double
    cream
1 egg yolk
milk, to dilute
a small handful or bunch of fresh
    herbs, such as parsley, basil or dill

Cook the fettucine in plenty of boiling salted water for about 8 minutes or until just tender. Meanwhile, heat the oil and butter in a frying pan, add the spring onions and fry over a low heat until softened. Add the smoked salmon shreds and turn rapidly to heat rather than cook. Beat the cream and egg yolk together and dilute to a runny consistency with a little milk. Add this to the salmon mixture, stir, and season generously with black pepper and a little salt. Remove from the heat. Drain the pasta and tip it into a warmed serving dish or bowl. Tip in the salmon mixture, plus the chopped herbs, and fork vigorously to mix well. Serve at once on warmed plates.

Spaghetti with Lumpfish Caviar and Crème Fraîche

A very quick and extravagant-seeming pasta dish. Though the roe is quite expensive (£1.40 for a small pot at time of going to press), this is one pasta dish which would be ruined by Parmesan (about £6.20 a pound) so there are no hidden extras. This is a good one to start a dinner party as there is really no work required and only one pan.

4 SERVINGS

500 g (1 lb) spaghetti (preferably egg
    spaghetti)
salt
a knob of butter

75 g (3 oz) crème fraîche or soured
    cream
50 g (2 oz) lumpfish caviar (red or
    black)

Cook the spaghetti in plenty of boiling salted water and have ready a warm serving dish. Drain the spaghetti when it is al dente and toss it with the butter. Pour into the hot serving dish and spoon the crème fraîche and then the lumpfish roe on top. Toss again at the table, so that every one can see the contrasting colours before they are blurred.

Aubergine and Pasta Timballo

Aubergines have a rich flavour and this pie is as satisfying as many meaty dishes.

4-6 SERVINGS

450 g (1 lb) tagliatelle
4 small aubergines
a pinch of salt
2 tablespoons olive oil for frying
450 g (1 lb) fresh tomatoes or
   1 medium can of peeled tomatoes
3 garlic cloves

50 g (2 oz) butter
black pepper
1 handful of fresh basil (or parsley,
   thyme or marjoram)
125 g (4 oz) Parmesan cheese, grated
4 tablespoons dried, home-made
   breadcrumbs

Cook the tagliatelle for 3–4 minutes so it is still firm. Drain and set aside in a warm place.

Thinly slice the unpeeled aubergines, salt lightly and leave for 10 minutes to sweat. Deep fry, a few slices at a time, in olive oil until golden brown, then drain on kitchen paper. Continue until all the aubergine is cooked.

Skin the tomatoes, remove the seeds, chop roughly and transfer to a colander to drain. Chop the garlic and lightly fry in a little oil and butter until golden, then add the tomato, salt and pepper and simmer for a few minutes. Chop the basil, minus stalks, or other herbs, quite finely. Mix the herbs, tomato mixture and grated cheese together with the cooked tagliatelle. Butter a deep cake tin generously (it must be big enough to take pasta and aubergines) and coat it evenly all over with breadcrumbs. Fill the dish with one layer of the pasta mixture, then one layer of aubergines, and so on until all the ingredients are used up. Top with more cheese, then breadcrumbs, then dot with butter and bake in a preheated oven at 220°C (425°F) mark 7 for 30 minutes. Turn on to a dish to serve.

N O T E : *For grand occasions you can substitute a pastry case, with lid, for the crumb case. Use shortcrust pastry (see page 71) and bake blind for 15 minutes. Cook a lid of the same pastry, decorated with pastry leaves, on a sheet of foil at the same time. Check after 10 minutes.*

Veggies

Vegetarian food needs no apology today, with eating habits evincing such a marked drift in the green direction, for reasons of health, economy and sentiment in varying measures. My family are not vegetarians, but like most of the people I know, we eat fewer meat meals a week than we used to, and many more which are either completely vegetarian or a compromise, in that they use some meat stock, or diced bacon, or leftover morsels of roast lamb or chicken, bulked up with rice or pasta.

Perhaps the happiest outcome of our change to a new, greener diet is that we have learnt, as a nation, to cook vegetables with proper respect, and imagination. *Nouvelle Cuisine* played a part in this evolution, as do the elegant assemblies of vegetables, cooked or raw, emanating from South–East Asia. Cashing in on the trend, shops, markets and supermarkets offer a profusion and variety of vegetables which would have been unthinkable 20 years ago outside Berwick Street market in Soho. In a picky mood, I might grumble that there is a certain sameness about much of the out–of–season produce – watery green peppers, floppy round lettuces, tasteless tomatoes – mostly raised in hydroponic greenhouses on Holland's light, sandy soil. And I agree with Italian cookery writer Anna del Conte that the practice of cooking

110

vegetables until *al dente* (tender but still slightly crisp) only, has gone too far. She claims that certain vegetables, notably asparagus, green beans, mange-touts, cauliflower and courgettes, are positively indigestible served *croquants* or crunchy. I certainly find the restaurant presentation of microwaved but undercooked vegetables, however prettily arranged, a damper on the appetite.

At the risk of seeming contrary, however, I am increasingly coming round to the view that finesse in preparation and cooking is all-important where vegetables are concerned. By finesse, I don't mean arty presentation so much as thoughtful treatment of each particular vegetable, designed to bring out its essential flavour and texture, and to make it look appetising. Nowadays, I always steam broccoli stalks for a few minutes ahead of the green florets, which so easily turn mushy. For years I sliced carrots and courgettes crossways, into discs; now I bother to cut them into matchsticks, because they actually taste better that way. I cook potatoes in their skins whenever possible because they retain so much more flavour. I undercook cabbage and spinach, drain and chop it, then toss quickly with butter, olive oil and chopped garlic.

The real inspiration for my own increasing interest in vegetables, and vegetable dishes, which may or may not be vegetarian, is the box of organically grown seasonal vegetables and herbs which arrives each week, ten months of the year, from a Suffolk garden. I never know what to expect – sheaves of chard, knobbly tomatoes, muddy celeriac, beetroots the size of marbles, white aubergines, purple basil, black salsify. Organic vegetables spoil fast, so it is a regular challenge to do justice to that week's delivery, but the bursting vitality of taste and texture almost straight from the soil is an unfailing reward, even if I do have to scrub off enough honest mud to plant a windowbox, and stuff the freezer with purées of this and that to prevent a surfeit of goodies going to waste. The delight of working with such excellent produce is that, after knocking oneself out trying to think of new and interesting recipes, one flops back on occasion to the simplest, most obvious solution in the world – a lick of butter and a grinding of pepper – and it's as if you are tasting them properly for the first time.

Lettuce and Pea Soup

6 SERVINGS

125 g (4 oz) butter	a large pinch of salt
1 lettuce, shredded	1 teaspoon sugar
900 g (2 lb) peas, shelled	1.1 litres (2 pints) water
a sprig of fresh mint	

Melt the butter in a large heavy-based saucepan, put in the lettuce, peas and mint with the salt and sugar, cover and cook gently for 10 minutes, stirring occasionally.

Add the water to the pan, turn up the heat and simmer with the lid off for 5-10 minutes or until the peas are tender. Leave the soup to cool slightly, then purée in a blender or food processor, or rub through a sieve. Return the soup to the pan and reheat gently before serving piping hot.

NOTE: *If possible, use a flavoursome type of lettuce for this soup, such as Cos or Little Gem.*

 ## Curried Parsnip Soup

6 SERVINGS

50 g (2 oz) butter
2 onions, chopped
2 teaspoons curry powder
450 g (1 lb) parsnips, peeled and
 diced
1 eating apple, peeled, cored and
 diced

1.1 litres (2 pints) water
salt and pepper
6 tablespoons crème fraîche, cream or
 yogurt, to serve
a sprig of fresh parsley or coriander,
 chopped

Melt the butter in a large heavy-based saucepan, add the onions and fry for about 5 minutes or until lightly coloured. Stir in the curry powder and fry for 1 minute. Add the parsnips and apple, cover and leave to sweat for 5-10 minutes, stirring occasionally. Add the water and simmer the soup for at least 30 minutes or until the parsnips are very tender (it won't hurt to keep them on the heat after they are ready). Leave the soup to cool slightly, then purée in a blender or food processor, or rub through a sieve. Return to the saucepan, season with salt and pepper, and reheat gently before serving with a spoonful of crème fraîche, cream or yogurt and a sprinkling of herbs for each diner.

Carrot and Coriander Soup

This soup has made my daughter Tabitha's reputation as a gastronome among her student pals. It is best made with vegetable stock, but an equal mixture of water and milk can be used instead.

4 SERVINGS

25 g (1 oz) butter
1 tablespoon vegetable oil
4 large carrots, peeled and grated
1 onion, finely chopped
1 litre (1¾ pints) vegetable stock

1 handful fresh coriander, finely
    chopped
salt and pepper
4 tablespoons single cream (optional)

Heat the butter and oil together in a large, heavy-based saucepan. Add the carrot and onion, cover, reduce the heat and leave to soften for 2-3 minutes. (This procedure considerably enriches any vegetable soup.)

Add the stock and simmer for 20-30 minutes. Add the coriander and cook for a further 2-3 minutes. Add salt and pepper to taste. Leave the soup to cool slightly, then purée in a blender or food processor. Return to the saucepan and reheat gently before serving in warmed individual bowls with a splash of cream added to each one if liked. Serve with hot bread or *crostini* (see page 134) for a light meal.

Chickpea and Lemon Soup

A good soup all the year round: the ingredients are always available and it's warming enough for winter and fresh enough for summer. Serve it on its own for a light lunch or supper with rolls and butter.

6 SERVINGS

200 g (7 oz) chickpeas
salt
3 tablespoons olive oil
1 large onion, finely chopped
3 garlic cloves, crushed
½-1 teaspoon cumin seeds

½ dried red chilli or ¼ teaspoon
    chilli powder
1 tablespoon tomato purée
1 teaspoon brown sugar
400 g (14 oz) can of tomatoes
grated rind and juice of 1 lemon

Soak the chickpeas in cold water for at least 3 or 4 hours, or overnight, then boil them in fresh water for about 1½ hours or until tender, salting them at the very end. Drain the chickpeas but do not throw away their cooking water. Heat the oil in a large heavy-based saucepan and fry the onion until it is transparent. Add the garlic and continue to fry for a few minutes.

Crush and grind the cumin seeds and chilli in a mortar, or in a strong bowl with the end of a rolling pin, and add to the onions and garlic. Cook for 1 minute. Pour in the chickpeas, heat through, then stir in the tomato purée and sugar. Pour over the canned tomatoes and bring to the boil. Make up the chickpea cooking water to 900 ml (1½ pints) with water and pour into the pan. Bring back to the boil, then reduce the heat and simmer for 10 minutes. Stir in the lemon rind and juice.

Broad Bean Soup

This is a useful emergency standby because it can be made from frozen broad beans. It needs to be puréed in a blender or food processor, or put through a mouli, to make a smooth soup, and you will need to add more stock, water or milk, to thin the soup after puréeing.

4 SERVINGS

2 tablespoons oil	1 teaspoon sugar
50 g (2 oz) butter	2 garlic cloves, chopped
1 large onion, chopped	a sprig of fresh thyme or savory
700 g (1½ lb) packet of frozen broad beans	500 ml (18 fl oz) vegetable stock
	extra stock, water or milk
400 g (14 oz) can of tomatoes	salt and pepper

Heat the oil and butter together in a large heavy-based saucepan, then add the onion, cover and sweat for about 5 minutes or until the onion is soft but not browned. Add the beans, tomatoes, sugar, garlic and thyme or savory, re-cover and simmer for 5-10 minutes or until the beans are thawed and tender, shaking the pan frequently.

Add the stock and simmer for a further 20-30 minutes. Leave to cool slightly, then purée by pressing through a sieve, or by processing in a blender or food processor, or put through a mouli to make a thick purée. Return to the saucepan and add more stock, milk or water to achieve the desired consistency. Reheat, season generously with salt and pepper, and serve in deep warmed bowls.

Crostini (see page 134) go well with this soup, for a light meal. Non-vegetarians might add diced unsmoked bacon with the beans. I sometimes add a soaked strand or two of saffron, for its glorious colour and aroma, but this is an extravagance.

Pappa Pomodoro (Bread and Tomato Soup)

Stale bread is never wasted in peasant cookery; the Tuscans serve it as *crostini*, or more nourishingly, as the thickening in this sturdy summer soup. The practice of using bread as thickening goes back to medieval times, but it must be good bread, *ciabbata* if you can get it, or stale white farmhouse, or best of all, Fleur Kelly's Roman Loaf (see page 180). Using sliced bread will produce a sticky, sloppy mush.

114

4 SERVINGS

4 slices of stale bread
600 ml (1 pint) vegetable stock
1-1½ × 400 g (14 oz) can of
   tomatoes
3 tablespoons olive oil

4 garlic cloves, chopped
salt and pepper
olive oil and lemon juice, to season
a handful of fresh basil, roughly torn

Tear the bread into pieces and soak it in the stock in a large saucepan until it is very soft. Drain the canned tomatoes, and fry in the oil with the garlic, mashing the tomatoes to break them into a purée. Continue to cook over a moderate heat until reduced to a thick, tasty purée. Season well with salt and pepper. Add the tomato mixture to the bread and stock, and heat through, stirring to mix. If the flavour needs boosting, add a spoonful or two more of olive oil, and a squeeze of lemon juice. Add the basil just before serving.

Tomatoes with Tzatziki

Tzatziki is a refreshing blend of cucumber and yogurt; it makes a pretty and complementary filling for halved, peeled tomatoes. The tomatoes should be ripe so this is best made when they are in season.

4-6 SERVINGS

1 medium cucumber
salt and pepper
150 g (5 oz) carton of natural yogurt
2 garlic cloves, finely chopped

2 tablespoons chopped fresh mint or
   coriander
4-6 ripe tomatoes
a little sugar

Peel the cucumber, cut it in half lengthways and scoop out the seeds with a teaspoon. Chop the cucumber quite small, put it in a sieve and sprinkle it with salt. Leave to stand for 20 minutes to draw out some of the moisture, then drain and mix with the yogurt. Add the garlic and mint or coriander, and season with salt and pepper.

Pour boiling water over the tomatoes, leave for 1 minute, or until the skins start to split, then drain, refresh under cold running water, and peel. Cut the tomatoes in half and scoop out the seeds to make cups. Sprinkle with sugar, salt and pepper, then fill each cup with the tzatziki. Serve alone, or with crisp lettuce leaves as a starter.

Coleslaw

Coleslaw is a very useful standby in winter, when the usual salad materials are expensive. Shredded raw cabbage – the hard, white type is the best – provides the bulk of the salad, and you can vary the other ingredients according to what you have in the way of vegetables. It is a good idea to make it an hour or so ahead, mix the dressing in and leave it standing.

4 SERVINGS

¼-½ white cabbage	2 celery sticks
1-2 carrots	½ small onion (optional)
1 large eating apple	French Dressing (see page 169)

Shred the cabbage as finely as possible with a sharp knife and leave it to crisp in a bowl of cold water while you prepare the rest of the ingredients. Peel and grate the carrots; peel, core and dice the apple; wash the celery and cut it into thin strips; grate or finely slice the onion. Dry the cabbage carefully and mix all the ingredients together. Dress with a French dressing to which you have added a little lemon juice, mustard and brown sugar.

VARIATIONS: I find a sprinkling of chopped fresh thyme – grown in a flowerpot on the windowsill – helps this salad. Dried thyme can be substituted, and you can throw in chopped walnuts, sultanas, grated cheese, shredded raw Brussels sprouts, shredded celeriac, and so on, as the fancy takes you.

New Potato Salad with Eggs, Peas and Mayonnaise

If you have mastered mayonnaise – and you should because even the best bottled is no substitute, as well as costing more – salads like this are splendidly tolerant and can be stretched to feed more faces by bumping up the potato and egg ratio, or adding some other ingredient to hand, such as cooked broad beans, or green beans, diced raw peppers, sliced radish and so on, not forgetting diced raw fruit, apple maybe, or a few chopped nuts. The staple ingredients are the waxy new potatoes, chopped spring onion, shallots or chives, a handful of herbs, the eggs and the mayonnaise.

116

4-6 SERVINGS
900 g (2 lb) smallish new potatoes
salt and pepper
6-10 eggs
1 bunch of spring onions, or 3
    shallots, or 1 bunch of chives
500 ml (18 fl oz) Mayonnaise (see
    page 170)

1 small packet of frozen peas (or
    broad beans)
fresh herbs, such as parsley, dill or a
    little basil, chopped
250 ml (8 fl oz) French Dressing
    (see page 169)

Scrub the potatoes, but do not peel them. Throw them into a large saucepan of boiling salted water and cook for 8–15 minutes, depending on size. If some are big, some tiny, add the tinies after 5 minutes, for parity. Meanwhile, put the eggs to cook. All hard–boiled eggs in my experience are best started in cold water, brought to the boil gradually, simmered for 4–5 minutes, then left in the water just to cool a little before being drained and peeled. This avoids green shadows and rubbery yolks, and makes for a bright and tender egg. While these are cooking, prepare and finely chop the shallots, spring onions or chives, and make the mayonnaise. When the potatoes are tender to the fork, drain and leave to cool a moment or two. Cook the frozen vegetables in a very little simmering water until just tender. Drain.

Peel the potatoes, wearing household gloves. Cooked potatoes peel quickly and cleanly, and taste better for being cooked in their skins. Combine the potatoes, shallots, peas, etc., and herbs in a bowl and anoint while warm with vinaigrette, adding salt and pepper to taste. Peel the eggs, slice them thickly and add. Dilute the thick mayonnaise by adding warm water slowly, beating after each slurp, until it reaches a thin cream consistency. When the salad has cooled somewhat (not steaming hot), pour on the mayonnaise, stir, toss (a bit gently) and serve, with a green, crunchy salad as ballast.

VARIATIONS: Acceptable extras include a few stoned black olives, a sprinkle of capers, one green chilli, very finely sliced, chopped walnuts or hazelnuts.

NOTE: *If such a quantity of mayonnaise alarms you, remember that you need not use olive oil alone. Use two parts olive oil to one of cheaper safflower or grapeseed oil and expect to dilute the thick, home-made article by as much as one third its volume with tepid water. This needs to be a fluid, mild mayonnaise.*

Braised Leeks

4 SERVINGS

450 g (1 lb) leeks
50 g (2 oz) butter or 2 tablespoons
   olive oil

a pinch of salt
a splash of red or white wine, or
   water

Trim and cut the leeks in quarters lengthways. Put them in a baking dish or casserole (preferably earthenware) which has a tight-fitting lid with the butter, or the oil, on top, a pinch of salt and the wine or water (plus a bit more if the leeks are not still a bit wet from washing). Cover tightly and cook in the oven at 180°C (350°F) mark 4 for about 30 minutes or until soft.

 ## Potatoes Cooked in Milk

Although time-consuming (as the potatoes must be stirred constantly), this is real 'comfort' food and is enough on its own for a light supper or lunch.

4 SERVINGS

700 g (1½ lb) potatoes, peeled and
   diced

568 ml (1 pint) milk
salt and black pepper

Put the potatoes in a heavy-based saucepan and pour over the milk. Bring to the boil over medium heat, then turn the heat right down. Season with salt and black pepper, and simmer, stirring constantly, for 25–30 minutes or until the potatoes are cooked.

 ## Leek and Potato Pie

4-6 SERVINGS

1 tablespoon plain flour
salt and pepper
freshly grated nutmeg
900 g (2 lb) potatoes, peeled and
   thinly sliced

4 leeks, trimmed and finely sliced
50-75 g (2-3 oz) butter
450 ml (¾ pint) hot milk

Season the flour with salt, pepper and nutmeg. Grease a baking dish or small casserole and put in alternate layers of potatoes and leeks, sprink-

118

ling each layer with the seasoned flour and dotting with butter. The top layer should be potatoes. Dot the top with more butter, pour over the hot milk and bake in the oven at 190°C (375°F) mark 5 for about 1 hour or until the vegetables are tender.

Baked Tomatoes

This is a delicious way to cook tomatoes as a vegetable dish. It keeps all their delicate natural flavour. You should use home-made bread-crumbs (see page 79). The kind sold in packets are not suitable.

4 SERVINGS

8-10 tomatoes, thickly sliced
salt and pepper
4 teaspoons brown sugar

125-175 g (4-6 oz) butter, cut into
tiny pieces
50 g (2 oz) breadcrumbs

Arrange the tomatoes in a shallow ovenproof dish. Season with salt and pepper, and sprinkle with the sugar. Dot with the butter and cover with breadcrumbs. Bake in the oven at 180°C (350°F) mark 4 for about 20 minutes.

'Hot' Greens

If you like chillies, try this fast way to perk up any of the rather more bitter green vegetables, such as spinach, Brussels sprouts tops, chard, land cress or spring greens. The quantities of chilli used are optional; one chilli may be as much as most people can take, but I like two, for a touch of fieriness. Remember to wash your hands well after handling chillies, and don't wipe your eyes or face until you have.

4 SERVINGS

900 g (2 lb) greens (see above)
4 tablespoons olive oil
1-2 dried red chillies, de-seeded and
  chopped

2 garlic cloves, chopped
salt and pepper

Pick over the greens, removing any tired-looking leaves or coarse stalks. Wash well and shake off most of the washing water. Put the greens in a large saucepan, cover and cook over a high heat until the leaves have wilted. Tip out on to a board and chop coarsely.

Heat the oil in a shallow pan, add the chilli and garlic and turn briefly, taking care not to burn the garlic. Add the greens and mix well to distribute the garlic, chilli and oil mixture evenly. Add salt and pepper to taste, then turn into a warmed dish and serve.

Orange-Glazed Carrots

4 SERVINGS

50 g (2 oz) butter
450 g (1 lb) carrots, peeled and cut
 into matchsticks

1 tablespoon brown sugar
175-250 ml (6-8 fl oz) water
juice of 1 orange

Melt the butter in a wide, heavy-based saucepan, put in the carrots and the sugar, and heat gently until the sugar has begun to melt. Pour over the water and bring to the boil, then turn down the heat and simmer for about 10 minutes or until the carrots are almost tender, adding a little more water if necessary. Pour in the orange juice and simmer until the juice has reduced to a rich glaze.

Spinach Soufflé

4 SERVINGS

225 g (8 oz) spinach
15 g (½ oz) butter, plus a small
 knob
1 tablespoon plain flour
150 ml (¼ pint) milk

40 g (1½ oz) Edam cheese, grated
2 large eggs, separated
salt and pepper
freshly grated nutmeg

Wash the spinach and trim off any tough-looking stalks. Put it in a pan with a small knob of butter and place a small heatproof plate or saucer upside-down on the pile of leaves to keep them near the source of the heat. Cover and cook over a high heat until the spinach has wilted. Drain and chop.

Melt the butter in a small saucepan, add the flour and cook, stirring, for 1-2 minutes. Remove from the heat and gradually add the milk, stirring constantly. Bring to the boil, stirring, and simmer until smooth and thick. Stir in the cheese until melted, then stir in the spinach and leave to cool slightly.

Beat in the egg yolks and season with salt, pepper and nutmeg. Beat the egg whites until stiff and fold them into the mixture. Turn the mixture into a buttered soufflé dish and cook in the oven at 190°C (375°F) mark 5 for about 20 minutes or until risen and brown on top.

Turnip Omelette

This recipe is a good example of everyday ingredients treated with sophisticated simplicity. It makes an excellent lunch or supper dish which needs only a green salad to keep it company.

2 SERVINGS

450 g (1 lb) small crisp turnips
salt and black pepper
50 g (2 oz) butter
4 eggs

a sprig of fresh parsley, finely
chopped
2 tablespoons olive oil

Cut the turnips into small cubes and sprinkle with salt. Put them in an omelette pan or small frying pan, preferably one with a handle that can go in the oven, with the butter and cook, stirring, for about 15 minutes or until the turnips are tender and slightly browned. Season with salt and pepper.

In a separate bowl, beat the eggs thoroughly with the parsley and season with a pinch of salt and plenty of black pepper. Pour the turnip mixture into the beaten egg and mix well. Clean the omelette pan, put the oil in it and heat. When the oil is hot, pour in the egg and turnip mixture, stir and flatten out the mixture in the pan. Cook for a minute over a high heat, then cook in the oven at 180°C (350°F) mark 4 for 5–10 minutes. If you have a pan which can't go in the oven, cook it for 5 minutes on each side under a moderate grill.

 # Rice with Broad Beans, Lemon and Herbs

4-6 SERVINGS

450 g (1 lb) easy-cook long-grain rice
salt and pepper
450 g (1 lb) shelled young broad
beans
2 tablespoons good olive oil

finely grated rind and juice of
1 lemon
a bunch of fresh coriander or chives,
finely chopped

Cook the rice in plenty of boiling salted water for about 10 minutes or until tender. Put the beans in a steamer or colander and place on top of

121

the boiling rice. Cover and steam for about 10 minutes or until just tender. Put the beans in a bowl and add the olive oil, lemon juice and lemon rind. Toss well to mix. Drain the rice and put it in a large serving bowl. Gently fold in the broad beans and herbs. Serve as part of a vegetarian feast.

 ## Sesame Rice

6-8 SERVINGS

2 teaspoons salt	4 teaspoons sesame seeds
450 g (1 lb) long-grain rice	2 teaspoons coriander seeds
1 teaspoon fenugreek seeds	1 teaspoon mustard seeds
1 teaspoon ground turmeric	50 g (2 oz) butter
1 teaspoon paprika	2 tablespoons unsalted peanuts
8 cardamom pods, lightly crushed	juice of 1 lemon

Put the salt in a large saucepan of water and bring to the boil. Add the rice and cook for 10-12 minutes.

Meanwhile, put all the seeds and spices, except the mustard seeds, in a frying pan with a knob of butter and heat gently for about 5 minutes or until roasted. Remove them from the pan and add the mustard seeds and peanuts to the pan. Fry until golden.

Drain the rice thoroughly and stir in the remaining butter. Add all the spices, seeds and nuts, sprinkle with lemon juice and mix thoroughly. Serve hot.

Pumpkin Risotto

6 SERVINGS

1 medium pumpkin, peeled and de-seeded	450 g (1 lb) easy-cook long-grain or arborio rice
1 tablespoon olive oil	900 ml (1½ pints) hot stock or water
140 g (4½ oz) butter	salt and black pepper
3 small onions or 4 shallots, sliced	grated Parmesan cheese

Cut the pumpkin into 2.5 cm (1 inch) cubes. Heat the oil and 125 g (4 oz) of the butter in a heavy-based frying pan large enough to hold the finished risotto. Add the onions or shallots and cook until softened, then put in the pumpkin. Cook the pumpkin and onions for 10 minutes, stirring, but don't let the onions burn. Pour in the rice. As soon as the rice is translucent, pour over a cupful of stock, cook until it has been absorbed, then pour over two more cupfuls and cook again.

Continue to add stock a cupful at a time until the rice and pumpkin are tender. Season with salt to taste and plenty of black pepper. Stir in the remaining butter and 1 tablespoon grated Parmesan. Serve immediately with more Parmesan on the table.

 ## Lentils with Basil

I am always curious to know what people who cook professionally like to make for themselves. This Italian recipe for lentils is a favourite with Sam Clark, *sous-chef* at the highly acclaimed Riverside Café in Hammersmith. He uses the tiny brown lentils sold in posher food stores and health food shops, but you can use the cheaper and more widely available green lentils also. When fresh basil is out of season, try a mixture of chopped spring onions (including some of the green part) and parsley.

4 SERVINGS

75 g (3 oz) brown or green lentils
3 large garlic cloves, crushed
juice of 1 large lemon
salt and freshly ground black pepper

4 tablespoons olive oil
a handful of fresh basil, finely
   chopped

Lentils do not need pre-soaking. Put them in a saucepan and cover with cold water by about 5 cm (2 inches). Add the garlic and bring gradually to the boil over a low heat. Simmer, uncovered, for 30–35 minutes or until the lentils are tender but not mushy. Check after 30 minutes. Drain the lentils, but not too thoroughly – a little cooking water will improve the texture of the dish. Turn the lentils into a serving dish and squeeze over the lemon juice. Add salt and lots of freshly ground black pepper, then the olive oil, turning with wooden forks (less bruising than spoons) until it glistens appetisingly. Add the chopped basil, mix well and serve hot, warm or cold, as a starter or as a salad or a *contorno*, or side dish, with a frittata, or with fried or grilled fresh sardines.

 ## Falafel

Excellent picnic food to eat with a salad dressed with yogurt, and pitta bread. Alternatively, it makes a good party dish served with rice and a hot tomato sauce. The remarkable thing about this chickpea recipe is that the chickpeas do not need to be boiled, making it economical on fuel.

8 SERVINGS

450 g (1 lb) chickpeas
2-4 small onions
4-5 garlic cloves
a sprig of fresh parsley or coriander
1 teaspoon cumin seeds

1 teaspoon coriander seeds
salt and pepper
1 teaspoon cayenne pepper
sunflower oil for frying

Soak the chickpeas in cold water overnight. Grind the chickpeas in a food mill, blender or food processor. If you are using a food processor, put the onions, garlic and parsley or coriander in with them. Otherwise, chop these finely and mix them into the ground chickpeas.

Grind the cumin and coriander seeds in a mill, or in a mortar, and stir them into the mixture. Season with salt, pepper and a little cayenne pepper. Continue working the mixture until it forms a rough paste, then form it into balls somewhere between the size of a walnut and a table tennis ball.

Pour about 5 mm (¼ inch) sunflower oil into a heavy-based frying pan and heat. When the oil is hot, add the falafel and fry them for about 15 minutes or until golden brown. Drain on absorbent kitchen paper before serving.

N O T E : *It may help to refrigerate the mixture for a while before forming it into balls.*

Daal

6 SERVINGS, OR MORE IF SERVED AS PART OF AN INDIAN
MEAL WITH OTHER DISHES

450 g (1 lb) yellow split peas or
  'Egyptian' lentils
1 tablespoon ground turmeric
5 cm (2 inch) piece of fresh root
  ginger, sliced but not peeled
1 small tablespoon salt
1 tablespoon garam masala
1 tablespoon coriander seeds

2 tablespoons cumin seeds
2 dried red chillies
6 tablespoons ghee or vegetable oil
3 onions, finely sliced
4 garlic cloves, sliced
1 sprig of fresh coriander, chopped
  (optional)

Wash the split peas or lentils and pick out any tiny stones or seeds. Put them in a large pan with about 2.3 litres (4 pints) water, the turmeric and ginger. Bring to the boil, then turn down the heat and simmer, partially covered, until the peas or lentils are tender (30 minutes to 1½ hours). When the daal is cooked, stir in the salt and garam masala.

In a pestle and mortar (you can improvise with a strong bowl and the end of a rolling pin), crush the coriander and cumin seeds until they are at least partially ground. You could do this in a coffee grinder if you have one. (Alternatively, if you don't fancy this stage at all, it will not be the end of the world if you use ready-ground spices, provided they are fresh. In this case, reduce the quantities to 1 teaspoon ground coriander and 2 teaspoons ground cumin.) Bruise the chillies slightly but do not let them split. In a large sauté or frying pan, heat the ghee or vegetable oil and put in the sliced onion, adding the garlic when the onion has just softened. When the onions are beginning to caramelise, add the spices and chillies. Let them sizzle for a few seconds and give off their aroma, then pour this hot spicy mixture over the daal and sprinkle the top with chopped fresh coriander if wished. Serve with brown or basmati rice and perhaps other Indian dishes.

Aubergine Toad-in-the-Hole

6 SERVINGS

2 large aubergines	a pinch of salt
salt	1 egg
2-6 garlic cloves, crushed	200 ml (7 fl oz) milk
olive oil for frying	100 ml (3 fl oz) water

FOR THE BATTER
125 g (4 oz) plain flour

Trim the ends off the aubergines, then halve the aubergines crossways and cut each half lengthways into sections as similar in shape to sausages as possible. Put the aubergine pieces in a colander, sprinkle them with salt and leave them for about 30 minutes to extract the bitter juices.

To make the batter, put the flour and salt in a bowl, make a well in the centre and add the egg and half the milk. Gradually work in the flour, stirring with a wooden spoon, then beat until smooth. Add the remaining milk and the water, and beat until well mixed and the surface is covered with tiny bubbles. Set aside.

Put the garlic and 4 tablespoons olive oil in a large heavy-based frying pan, preferably one with a handle that can go in the oven. Drain the aubergine pieces, rinse them and pat dry with absorbent kitchen paper. When the oil is hot, add the aubergine pieces and fry them for about 20 minutes or until golden. They will first absorb the oil, then melt it back into the pan as they cook. Remove the aubergine from the pan with a slotted spoon, place the pieces on a warmed plate and keep warm.

Add some more oil to the pan, if necessary, and when it is hot, re-move the pan from the heat and pour in the batter. Place the aubergine pieces in the batter, arranging them evenly in the pan. Bake in the oven at 220°C (425°F) mark 7 for 40–45 minutes or until the pudding is risen and golden.

 ## Gratin of Courgettes

Gratin is a French name given to a mixture of lightly pre-cooked veget-ables (courgettes here, but green beans, chicory slices, Swiss chard and broccoli are all equally suitable), bound with eggs, enriched with grated cheese and fresh herbs, and baked until it is transformed into a sort of solid vegetable cake, excellent with a crisp salad and perhaps a fresh tomato sauce. Leftover cooked vegetables can also be re-cycled as a gratin (in fact, I suspect this is how the idea originated) but make a little extra effort to trim and chop the vegetables for an appetising effect. Cheddar cheese can be substituted for pricy Parmesan or Gruyère. Rice adds substance.

4 SERVINGS

900 g (2 lb) small, firm courgettes,
   sliced into rounds or matchsticks
salt and pepper
4 tablespoons olive oil
2 large onions, chopped
2 garlic cloves, chopped

3 eggs, plus 1 egg yolk
75 g (3 oz) Parmesan, Gruyère or
   mature Cheddar cheese, grated
3-4 tablespoons cooked long-grain
   white or brown rice

Put the courgettes in a colander, salt lightly and leave for 30 minutes to extract the juices.

Heat 1 tablespoon oil in a frying pan, add the onion and garlic, cover and cook over a low heat for about 5 minutes or until soft but not burned. Remove the onions and garlic from the pan, wipe out the pan, add 2 tablespoons oil, and, when hot, add the courgettes. Cover and cook for 10-15 minutes or until softened.

Break the eggs into a large bowl, add the extra yolk, and beat with a fork. Add 50 g (2 oz) grated cheese and the cooked rice and season with salt and pepper. Mix in the softened onions, garlic and courgettes. Oil a shallow gratin dish and tip in the vegetable mixture. Drizzle the re-maining oil on top, sprinkle with the remaining grated cheese, then bake in the oven at 180°C (350°F) mark 4 for about 30 minutes or until solid enough to cut with a knife, and lightly browned on top. Serve warm, rather than hot. Excellent picnic food.

Ratatouille

This must be a cornerstone of any vegetarian diet – good to look at, good to eat, versatile and blessedly easy to make. It is not the sort of dish where quantities are critical; you can use more courgettes, less or no aubergine, various peppers, fresh or canned tomatoes. It always seems to come out right, succulent and colourful. I like mine quite juicy so I don't skimp on tomatoes. As well as being delicious warm or cold, on its own with a slice of coarse bread, it makes a fine companion to a frittata, or a bowl of small new potatoes with aïoli. When you are getting down to the bottom of the pot, spread a layer of ratatouille over the bottom of an ovenproof dish, break in an egg or two per head, drizzle with oil, cover with foil and bake in the oven at 180°C (350°F) mark 4 until the eggs are just set – about 12 minutes.

5-6 SERVINGS

1 medium aubergine
salt and pepper
250 ml (8 fl oz) olive oil
700 g (1½ lb) onions, roughly
    chopped
450 g (1 lb) peppers, green, red or
    yellow, or a mélange, de-seeded
    and cut into strips
750 g (1½ lb) ripe tomatoes, skinned
    and chopped, or 2 × 400 g
    (14 oz) can of peeled tomatoes

5 garlic cloves, chopped
1 sprig each of fresh thyme, rosemary
    and parsley
1 bay leaf
450 g (1 lb) courgettes, sliced
chopped fresh parsley, to serve

If you can cook the ratatouille in an earthenware pot, do, because it not only looks nicer but seems to taste richer. Use a heat diffuser mat between the pot and the hotplate or gas ring. Start by preparing the aubergine. Cut it into dice and stand it in a colander. Sprinkle with salt to extract the bitterness.

Heat the oil in an earthenware pot or saucepan and cook the onion, covered, over a low heat for about 8 minutes or until softened. Add the aubergine and peppers, and cook for another 10 minutes, stirring now and then, over low heat. When these are softening, add the tomatoes, garlic, herbs, and a little salt and pepper. Canned tomatoes add more liquid than fresh, so add water in the latter case; ratatouille should start cooking with plenty of juice. Simmer, half covered, for about 1 hour. Add the courgettes, and cook for another 30 minutes or until the courgettes are tender. If the liquid seems insufficient, stir in some warm water. Taste and adjust the seasoning. A sprinkle of fresh parsley on top is traditional.

Spanakopitta

This classic Greek pie of spinach baked with cheese in layers of papery filo pastry is so good that every vegetarian cook should know it by heart. Packets of frozen filo pastry are obtainable in most supermarkets and delicatessens, and make the preparation simplicity itself. Spinach tastes mysteriously nicer if you tear the leaves with your fingers instead of chopping them.

6 SERVINGS

900 g (2 lb) spinach
250 g (9 oz) feta cheese, crumbled
salt and pepper

1 packet frozen filo pastry, thawed
4 tablespoons melted butter or olive oil

Wash the spinach thoroughly in cold water, drain in a colander, then tear into pieces, discarding any tough stalks. Put the spinach in a large saucepan, cover and cook over a high heat for just long enough to wilt the leaves. Drain the spinach and put it in a bowl with the cheese. Mix lightly and season with salt and pepper.

Oil or butter a shallow earthenware gratin dish. (A square dish makes laying out the filo sheets easier, but a round or oval one can be used.) Brush about six sheets of filo pastry with melted butter or oil and use to line the dish, allowing flaps of pastry to hang over all the sides. Spread this with half the spinach and cheese mixture. Butter or oil some more sheets of filo and lay these on top, then pour the rest of the spinach in. Fold all the loose flaps of filo over to make a nice neat parcel, adding another sheet or two, if necessary.

Brush the top of the pie with more butter or oil, then bake in the oven at 180-190°C (350-375°F) mark 4-5 for 30-40 minutes or until the pastry is golden. Cover with a loose piece of foil if the pie is browning too fast. Remove from the oven and turn the pie out on to a plate, then slide it back into the dish, upside-down, and cook in the oven for another 10 minutes or until the bottom is golden. Best served warm; good with a tomato salad.

Curried New Potatoes in their Jackets

New potatoes, cooked with spices in the Indian manner, are a treat, substantial enough for a main dish served with a daal, and cachumbar, the chunky Indian salad of tomato, cucumber and lettuce. Ghee (clarified butter) makes it much richer and does not catch and burn like ordinary butter.

4-6 SERVINGS

75 g (3 oz) ghee (or use vegetable oil)
1 large onion, finely chopped
1 heaped teaspoon ground turmeric
700 g (1½ lb) very small new potatoes, scrubbed

2 green chillies, de-seeded and finely chopped
salt
250 g (8 oz) packet of frozen peas, thawed
2 teaspoons garam masala

Heat the ghee or oil in a saucepan wide enough to take all the potatoes in one layer. Add the onion, cover and fry for about 5 minutes or until soft and just golden. Add the turmeric, stir and cook for 1 minute, then add the potatoes, chilli and salt. Cook for 5 minutes, shaking the pan from time to time. Turn the heat right down, cover and cook for 20 minutes or until the potatoes are almost done. Add the peas, sprinkle over the garam masala, shake again and cook for a further 10 minutes.

Potato and Pea Curry

Coconut milk can be bought in tins or as a powder to which you add water. If you cannot find it, use dairy milk instead.

6 SERVINGS

700 g (1½ lb) potatoes, scrubbed
25 g (1 oz) butter
1 onion, chopped
5 cm (2 inch) piece of fresh root ginger, peeled and chopped
a sprig of fresh coriander, chopped
1 teaspoon ground turmeric

½ teaspoon ground coriander
½ teaspoon chilli powder
450 g (1 lb) shelled fresh or frozen peas
a pinch of salt
300 ml (½ pint) coconut milk
1 teaspoon garam masala

Cook the potatoes in boiling water for 8–10 minutes or until they are half cooked. Drain, leave until cool, then peel and roughly chop.

Melt the butter in a frying pan and fry the onion, ginger and coriander for 5–10 minutes or until the onion is golden. Add the dry spices, except the garam masala, and continue to fry for a further 4 minutes. Stir in the potatoes, peas and salt. Add the coconut milk and garam masala, cover and simmer for about 15 minutes or until the potatoes are cooked.

Fancy Work

The food in this chapter is intended to be slightly out of the ordinary in one way or another – more extravagant, more elaborate, or more exotic. For these reasons, I think of it as food for special occasions, rather than every day. You can please yourself as to what occasions you choose to call special – dinner party, anniversary, seduction scene, peace offering or simply a break in humdrum routine for the cook. Your choice of food depends on the circumstances. Jiaozi (Peking Dumplings) would be a mistake at a rather stiff gathering of people, where your presence, all smiles and unruffled charm, is needed to keep things moving at all. A largely cold meal, which can be prepared ahead, with one hot dish needing very last-minute attention, is in order here. Crostini, Baked Gammon and perhaps Steamed Lemon Mousse would be a good choice. Greedy friends of long standing, on the other hand, will enjoy all the brouhaha of making the above-mentioned dumplings, and probably give you a hand as well. Something light and elegant seems to be indicated for romantic evenings, unless instinct tells you that you are dealing with a massive appetite. Almost all men can be appeased by platefuls of hot and fiery food – provide plenty of cold beer or lager to wash it down with.

Paupers are probably debarred by lack of cash from giving as many

131

duty dinners (to impress the boss, rich relations, chance celebrities) as other people. Still, such occasions crop up from time to time and cause a disproportionate amount of anxious planning and brooding and fussing about what to eat, and what to drink, and what will they like and/or be impressed by. The rule in such cases is – don't over-reach yourself. Better to provide them with an unpretentious dish you know you can cook well, without agony of mind, than something untried which sounds very grand and costs so much you have to rely on the cheapest of wines to lubricate the conversation. (Rule 2 – you can offer cider or plonk to your friends, but never to the other category of guests. If you can't afford at least two bottles of a reasonable wine, it would be wiser to put the evening off.) If you wish to impress, don't try to be impressive. A pleasant soup to start off with, followed by a handsome-looking pie or Steak and Kidney Pudding (this homely classic has acquired considerable class, perhaps because so many people have forgotten how to make it) with appropriate vegetables (again for snob reasons, boiled sprouts score over frozen peas). Some frothy-looking confection to end up with (Dur Mou, Orange Jelly), quite a lot of some pleasant wine to wash it all down, and your evening of strategic socialising is off to a good start. The effect to aim for is home-made food as it was in the good old days, simple, well cooked, and a far cry from the tarted up stuff they eat at expense-account lunches.

Gazpacho

Cold, highly spiced Spanish soup. If you own an electric blender, you can whizz through the preparation in a few minutes. Otherwise, you will have to use a mouli, comforting yourself with the thought that most Spanish cooks still pound up the ingredients in a mortar or chop them interminably until they are reduced to a pulp.

4 SERVINGS

½ cucumber, peeled and chopped
1 large onion, chopped
450 g (1 lb) tomatoes, skinned, de-seeded and chopped
1 garlic clove, crushed
1 green pepper, de-seeded and chopped
540 ml (19 fl oz) can of tomato juice

cayenne pepper, to taste
2-3 tablespoons lemon juice or wine vinegar or a mixture
4-6 tablespoons olive oil
salt (optional)
ice cubes and croûtons (see page 29), to serve

Reserve a little cucumber, onion and tomato to serve with the soup. Purée all the remaining vegetables in a blender (with a little of the

132

tomato juice) or mouli, or chop them all together very finely on a board. Mix with the tomato juice, cayenne, vinegar or lemon juice and olive oil. It is probably best to add the last two ingredients a bit at a time, tasting frequently, to make sure the soup is neither too acid nor too oily. Add a little salt if necessary. Chill well.

Serve in bowls with an ice cube floating in each one. Guests help themselves to raw diced vegetables and croûtons.

Wonton Soup

This is a favourite with children but you may want to omit the chilli and go easy on the garlic and ginger – the quantities given below are designed for adult tastes.

8 SERVINGS

6 garlic cloves, skinned

5 cm (2 inch) piece of fresh root ginger, peeled

225 g (8 oz) minced pork

a sprig of fresh coriander or parsley, finely chopped

1 fresh or dried red chilli, de-seeded and very finely chopped

soy sauce, to taste

salt and black pepper

1 small packet of wonton wrappers (about 30)

900 ml (1½ pints) chicken stock, made with a 2.5-5 cm (1-2 inch) piece of root ginger (see page 21)

a bunch of spring onions, thinly sliced

sesame oil, to taste (optional)

Chop together the garlic and ginger, and mix with the minced pork and coriander or parsley. Add the chilli and season with soy sauce, salt and pepper. Put a small amount of the mixture on each wonton wrapper and twist to close.

Put the chicken stock in a saucepan and bring to simmering point. Drop in the wontons and spring onions and simmer for about 5 minutes. Season to taste with soy sauce and sesame oil, if using, then pour into individual bowls and serve immediately.

Devils on Horseback

A wintry treat to serve with drinks, or as a starter or 'savoury', or as an accompaniment to roast fowl.

MAKES 12

12 prunes

hot tea or water for soaking

6 teaspoons chutney

12 rashers of streaky bacon, de-rinded and trimmed of excess fat

133

Soak the prunes for 30 minutes in hot tea or water. Drain them, then remove the stones and fill each cavity with ½ teaspoon chutney. Wrap a rasher of bacon around each prune and secure with wooden cocktail sticks. Place on a baking sheet and cook in the oven at 200°C (400°F) mark 6 for about 20 minutes or until the bacon is cooked. Serve hot.

  ## 'Seaweed'

4 SERVINGS

450 g (1 lb) spring greens or green
   cabbage, trimmed
peanut (groundnut) or other light oil
   for deep frying

2 teaspoons caster sugar
½ teaspoon salt
a pinch of monosodium glutamate
   (optional)

Wash the spring greens or cabbage leaves carefully, then cut into the thinnest possible strips. Spread them out on a clean cloth and leave to dry for a few hours, or overnight.

Heat the oil and deep-fry the strips of leaves in batches for 2 minutes or until darker green and crisp. Drain on kitchen paper and toss with the sugar, salt and monosodium glutamate, if using.

 ## Crostini

4-6 SERVINGS

50 g (2 oz) can of anchovies, drained
milk for soaking
1 French bread stick
225 g (8 oz) chicken livers, thawed
   if frozen

2 tablespoons olive oil
2 garlic cloves, crushed
75-125 ml (3-4 fl oz) wine
2 tablespoons capers, drained

Put the anchovies in a bowl, cover with milk and leave to soak. Cut the bread diagonally into long slices, place on a baking sheet and bake in the oven at 190°C (375°F) mark 5 until golden.

Clean the chicken livers and chop into large pieces. Heat the olive oil in a heavy-based frying pan and fry the chicken livers and garlic until the livers are browned but not overcooked. Add the wine for the last minute. Leave to cool slightly, then put in a food processor with the capers. Drain the anchovies and add them to the mixture, then process until finely chopped. Alternatively, combine everything on a board and chop finely. Spread on the French bread slices and serve at once.

Tapenade

Tapenade is a sort of relish, salty and pungent, much eaten in Provence. You can spread it on thin slices of toast, eat it with cheese, on biscuits, even stuff hard-boiled eggs with it. If you like the taste of olives, you will love it. It would be a good appetiser before a meal, a change from taramasalata made with pounded cod's roes. You will need a pestle and mortar, or a very strong bowl and the end of a rolling pin, for the preparation.

6-8 SERVINGS

125 g (4 oz) black olives, pitted and chopped
125 g (4 oz) green olives, pitted and chopped
10 anchovy fillets, drained

1 tablespoon capers, drained and chopped
1 hard-boiled egg yolk
a little chopped fresh or dried thyme
olive oil, to moisten

Put the olives in a mortar and pound to a paste. Add the anchovy fillets and pound until smooth. Add the capers and egg yolk and pound until smooth. Add the thyme and a trickle of olive oil and mix well. The tapenade should not be liquid, just moist enough to spread easily, so add only enough oil to achieve this consistency. Pack into a small jar.

 # Kipper Paste

4-6 SERVINGS

1 pair of traditional undyed kippers
about 125 g (4 oz) unsalted butter, softened

1 tablespoon lemon juice
salt, cayenne pepper and ground mace, to taste

Pour boiling water over the kippers and leave for 10 minutes, then drain, skin and bone them. Weigh the flesh, then flake it and beat in an equal weight of butter. Add the lemon juice. Season with ground mace, cayenne pepper and extra salt if you think it needs it. Serve with slices of hot toast.

Leeks Vinaigrette

Serve these cold, either as an hors d'oeuvre, or with cold meat or chicken. Choose leeks as near as possible the same size.

2 SERVINGS

4 leeks	freshly grated nutmeg
salt and pepper	French Dressing (see page 169)

Wash the leeks carefully – steeping them upside down in cold water helps to loosen the mud and grit – and trim them to roughly the same length, leaving an inch or so of green on each one. Plunge them into boiling salted water, and boil, covered, until tender but not mushy. The time depends on the size of the leeks – prod them with a fork to test them. Drain them very thoroughly in a colander, finishing off by patting them dry with absorbent kitchen paper. Sprinkle them with a little salt, pepper and nutmeg, and douse with French dressing. Leave to get cold.

Baked Chicken Liver Salad

This can be served for a light lunch or supper, or as a dinner–party starter.

4 SERVINGS

225 g (8 oz) chicken livers	1 teaspoon whole grain mustard
3 tablespoons olive oil	a salad of strong-flavoured and bitter
1 teaspoon black pepper	leaves – spinach, Cos lettuce,
1 teaspoon paprika	rocket, radicchio, dandelion,
2 garlic cloves, finely chopped	chicory – any one or a
salt	combination of these would be
2 tablespoons vinegar (wine, sherry or balsamic)	suitable
125 g (4 oz) streaky bacon, de-rinded and cut into thin strips	

Trim the chicken livers of any green or sinewy parts. Put them in a bowl with 2 tablespoons olive oil, the pepper, paprika and garlic, and marinate for at least 1 hour (overnight won't hurt).

Lay the oily livers on a baking sheet, sprinkle with salt and bake in the oven at 200°C (400°F) mark 6 for 20 minutes, pouring 1 tablespoon vinegar over them 5 minutes before the end of the cooking time. Heat the bacon in a dry, heavy-based frying pan over a gentle heat. (Always cook streaky bacon over gentle heat with no extra fat – this allows it to shed the water which factory bacon so often has in it, and gives its fat time to melt, banishing that dreaded rubbery texture.) When the bacon is crispy, turn off the heat and stir in the remaining olive oil and vinegar, and the mustard. Pour the baked livers and crispy bacon bits over the salad.

Smoked Mackerel, Radicchio and Hot Potato Salad

4-6 SERVINGS

450 g (1 lb) new potatoes, scrubbed
1 smoked mackerel
1 small head of radicchio
1 onion, finely chopped

FOR THE DRESSING

75 ml (3 fl oz) olive or hazelnut oil
1 tablespoon white wine vinegar
½ teaspoon mustard powder
salt and pepper

Cook the potatoes in boiling salted water for 15-20 minutes or until tender. Meanwhile, remove the skin and bones from the mackerel and cut the fish into even slices. Tear the radicchio leaves into manageable pieces. Make up the dressing by beating the ingredients together in a bowl.

When the potatoes are ready, drain them, cut them up roughly and put them back in the warm pan. Place over a high heat and very quickly throw in the onion, radicchio and dressing. After just a few seconds, turn the salad into a bowl, throw on the mackerel pieces and serve immediately.

Swedish-Style Marinated Herrings

This must be made with the freshest herrings, bright-eyed and firm as cucumbers. An obliging fishmonger will fillet them for you. Then all you need do is cut them diagonally into neat strips and marinate them in this sweet and spicy Swedish-inspired 'cure' for 48 hours or so. I find standard roll-mop marinades harshly vinegary; the Scandinavian additions of sugar, mustard and spices transform this into an elegant and unusual starter, served with half a hard-boiled egg, a slice of dark rye bread and Curry Mayonnaise (see page 138). A thimbleful of ice cold aquavit, or schnapps if you can afford it, is the perfect chaser.

6-8 SERVINGS

4 very fresh herrings, filleted and de-
scaled
FOR THE MARINADE
about 500 ml (18 fl oz) white wine
vinegar
1 tablespoon mild French mustard,
eg Dijon

2 teaspoons fresh coriander seeds,
slightly bruised in a mortar
1 tablespoon soft brown sugar
1 teaspoon salt
1 tablespoon finely chopped fresh dill
(optional but nice)

Combine all the marinade ingredients in a bowl and stir to mix well and dissolve the sugar. Arrange the strips of fish, skin side out, in a glass jar, piling them up in an overlapping spiral. Pour over the 'cure', cover the jar and stand in a cool place for 2–4 days. To serve, lay the strips on plates with hard-boiled egg halves and dark bread for contrast, and pass round Curry Mayonnaise (see below) separately.

 ## Curry Mayonnaise

The chef at one of my favourite restaurants (The Spread Eagle in Greenwich) serves this mayonnaise with sweet-cured herring (see above).

6-8 SERVINGS

2 egg yolks
1 tablespoon Dijon mustard
salt
a pinch of cayenne pepper
500 ml (18 fl oz) vegetable oil,
preferably mild-tasting safflower
or grapeseed oil

½–1 teaspoon Madras curry paste
½ tablespoon white wine vinegar
a squeeze of lemon juice (optional)

Whisk the egg yolks, mustard, salt and cayenne pepper together in a bowl. Add the oil a drop at a time, whisking constantly, until the mixture begins to come together in a glossy lump. At this point, you can add the oil in splashes, but continue whisking until the oil is all incorporated. Stir the curry paste into the vinegar and add to the mayonnaise, whisking to blend well. Taste and adjust the seasoning, adding a squeeze of lemon juice, if liked. If the mayonnaise is too thick, 1–2 tablespoons warm water can be whisked in to lighten it.

N O T E : *This mayonnaise has many other uses: as a dip for crudités; with poached fish; or in a potato salad.*

Stuffed Mussels

An appetising way of serving mussels as a light first course. You can use less garlic if you prefer.

4 SERVINGS

1.1 litres (2 pints) fresh mussels
50 g (2 oz) butter
about 3 tablespoons dry breadcrumbs
3 garlic cloves, finely chopped
a handful of fresh parsley, finely
    chopped

salt and black pepper
1 teaspoon grated lemon rind
a little white wine (optional)

First clean the mussels thoroughly. Rinse them under running water to remove grit or weed. Pull off the beards with pliers or a strong knife. Discard any mussels that refuse to close. Rinse again. Put the mussels in a saucepan large enough to take them in one layer on the bottom. Place the pan over moderate heat, with the cover on, and cook for 1-2 minutes or until the mussels have opened. Discard any mussels that do not open at all. Half-open is enough. If the mussels are overcooked at this stage, they will be tough. Strain any liquid off into a bowl and remove one shell from each mussel.

Melt the butter in a frying pan and gently fry the breadcrumbs and garlic, stirring until the crumbs are soft and have absorbed the butter. Remove from the heat and mix in the parsley, a little salt, black pepper and the grated lemon rind. Arrange the mussels in a shallow ovenproof dish and spread a little stuffing over each one. Pour over the mussel liquor, and a splash of white wine, if you have any. Cook in the oven at 190°C (375°F) mark 5 for 5-10 minutes or until the mussels are heated through. Serve at once.

 ## Mussels in Black Bean Sauce with Coriander

Fermented black bean sauce, from any good supermarket, is a bit like the Chinese equivalent of brown sauce, with a pungent, salty-sweet base which goes wonderfully well with seafood. The addition of ginger, garlic and coriander gives this mussel dish an authentic and mind-blowing fragrance.

4 SERVINGS

1 kg (2 lb) mussels
1 tablespoon peanut or other
  vegetable oil
a small knob of fresh root ginger,
  peeled and finely chopped

2 garlic cloves, chopped
2-3 tablespoons black bean sauce
a small handful of fresh coriander,
  chopped together with 3 spring
  onions

Wash and scrape the mussels and pull off the beards with a small, sharp knife. Throw out any mussels that are not tightly closed. Heat the oil in a heavy-based saucepan, add the ginger, garlic and mussels, cover and cook over a brisk heat for 2 minutes, then check whether the mussels are opening. Catch them as soon as possible after they open as prolonged heat toughens them.

Meanwhile, pound the bean sauce to a smooth paste in a mortar. Add it to the mussels and give the pan a good shake to mingle the bean paste with the mussel liquor. Scatter chopped coriander and spring onions on top and serve in bowls or soup plates, with a big dish to put the shells in.

Grilled Squid with Chilli, Parsley and Garlic Sauce

This makes an elegant and colourful starter. Each diner has a few pieces of the crispy squid which he or she dips into the green or red sauce.

4-6 SERVINGS

450 g (1 lb) small squid, thawed if
  frozen
1 large or 2 small fresh green or red
  chillies, de-seeded and very finely
  chopped

6 garlic cloves, very finely chopped
a bunch of fresh flat-leafed parsley or
  coriander, very finely chopped
150 ml (¼ pint) olive oil

To clean fresh squid, rinse it thoroughly, then pull on the head and tentacles until the soft contents of the body slip out. Cut the tentacles off just in front of the eyes. Discard the body contents and the head. Remove the semi-transparent quill from inside the body and rinse the body inside and out, rubbing it with your fingertips to remove any white substance and the fine, dark outer skin. Cut the body pouch into strips and the tentacles into bunches. Score the strips on one side with a knife.

Put the chilli, garlic and parsley or coriander in a mortar and crush together with the pestle, or use a very strong bowl and the end of a

140

rolling pin. Stir in the olive oil to make a thick sauce. Put 1 tablespoon of the sauce in a bowl, stir in the squid and leave to marinate for at least 30 minutes.

Cook the squid under a medium grill for 5-10 minutes or until it turns stiff and opaque, turning once. Serve with the remaining sauce.

Seafood Dumplings (Ravioli)

This recipe is inspired by one in Frances Bissell's *The Pleasures of Cookery*. I have made it pauperish by substituting some prawns for scallops, and editing the presentation. What we end up with here is about six semi-circular pasta dumplings per person, with a delectable fishy stuffing, sitting in a pool of fragrant sauce. It is not often I embark on home-made ravioli but the excellence of this combination justifies the toil, not major in this case as your guests get only a few (though surprisingly filling) ravioli each. I used to think of this as a starter for an occasion where to please/impress is important, but by increasing quantities as I suggest you have a superb main dish. Do budget for the saffron. I know it is an extravagance, but it adds real glamour. Buy it powdered, in sachet form, from Italian delis.

6 SERVINGS

225 g (8 oz) Home-made Fresh Pasta (see page 99)
FOR THE FILLING AND SAUCE
600 ml (1 pint) prawns in their shells

1 sachet powdered saffron
6 shallots, finely chopped
2 large scallops
salt and pepper
1 tablespoon finely chopped dill

Shell the prawns and put the shells in a saucepan with the saffron. Cover with cold water and simmer for 20 minutes. Strain off the debris, return the liquid to the pan, add the chopped shallots and simmer for another 5 minutes. Drain through a fine sieve into a bowl, reserving both stock and shallots. Separate the corals from the white parts of the scallops, and cut off the thin dark ring round the white meat, plus the little tough pad of muscle. Chop the raw scallops, corals and peeled prawns to a coarse mush. Season lightly with salt and pepper and mix in half the reserved blanched shallots and a pinch of chopped dill.

Roll out the pasta as thinly as possible, and stamp into rounds with a wine glass. Cover the pasta with a damp tea-towel while making the ravioli. Put a heaped teaspoon of filling on each pasta circle, fold over and wet the edges with water before pressing firmly together. Lay these on a floured tea-towel and cover with another dampened tea-

141

towel as you complete them. Do all this ahead, the afternoon of the party; the ravioli will be fine under a dampened cloth for a couple of hours. Continue until you have used up all the filling.

The sauce can also be prepared ahead. Boil up the prawn stock with the remaining reserved shallots until reduced by a third to a half. It should taste concentrated and look deep golden. Add the remaining chopped dill, and season to taste.

Allow 5 minutes to get the ravioli and sauce on to the table from the time the pan boils. Put serving plates in the oven to heat. Bring the sauce back to simmering. Bring a large, wide pan of water to the boil and drop in the ravioli, in two batches if necessary. Cook for 3 minutes, then remove with a slotted spoon. Spoon a little sauce on to each warmed plate and add some ravioli. Serve as quickly as possible.

It would be a mistake to clutter up such a special dish with extras; start the meal with a vivid soup, such as gazpacho or borshch, served with hot crusty bread, and finish up with a green salad and cheese, or fresh fruit and cheese.

Koulibiac

This is a trusty party recipe – it looks spectacular as pies will, and it has the great virtue of being as good cold as hot, so you can prepare it a day beforehand, and it makes extravagant ingredients go a long way - so that though your guests will feel you've gone to town you won't in fact be over-paupering yourself. Though it is traditionally made with salmon, I've tried this pie with less grand kinds of fish – smoked haddock gave it a good colour and interesting flavour. Served with plenty of salad, this dish will serve 12; more as part of a buffet with another main dish.

12 SERVINGS

FOR THE PASTRY
700 g (1½ lb) strong white flour
2 teaspoons salt
1 packet fast action dried yeast
2 eggs
3 tablespoons olive or sunflower oil
1 egg, beaten, to glaze
FOR THE FILLING
6 tablespoons millet, rinsed
salt and pepper

a pinch of ground turmeric
3 onions, chopped
butter for frying
225 g (8 oz) mushrooms, chopped
450 g (1 lb) salmon fillets or a
   mixture of salmon and smoked
   haddock
4 eggs, hard-boiled and chopped
a large bundle of fresh dill, parsley or
   chervil, finely chopped

142

Make the yeast pastry by pouring the flour into a mixing bowl. Stir in the salt and the yeast, break in the eggs and pour in the oil. Add enough cold water gradually to make a smooth dough. Leave to rise in a warm place for about 45 minutes.

Toast the damp millet in a dry pan until it begins to give off a nutty smell. Put it to boil in plenty of boiling salted water, with the turmeric, until it is tender but not soggy. Drain and rinse under cold running water and leave in the sieve to drain thoroughly. Fry the onions gently in butter until they are just softened, put in the chopped mushrooms and continue to fry gently until they yield up their moisture. Turn the onions and mushrooms into a dish and leave to cool. Put another knob of butter in the pan (there is no need to wash it) and gently cook the salmon fillets (grind some black pepper and a fraction of salt over them) – just until they are firm and the colour has lightened. Remove them from the pan and put on another plate. Leave to cool.

When the dough has doubled in size, knock it back and knead it briefly. Remove a nugget for decorating the finished pie with. Flour the table, your hands and whatever you are using as a rolling pin and roll the dough out to as large a rectangle as will fit your baking sheet, or two smaller ones. The dough should be fairly elastic and you might be able to make a pie with a very fine crust, but about 0.5 cm (¼ inch) thickness is probably a safe thickness to work with for your first try.

Lay half the millet down the middle of your rectangle (or a quarter down the middle of each, and so on), leaving enough margin to fold up round the sides and at the ends. Season with salt and pepper and lay half the mushroom and onion mixture over the millet. Season again with a little salt and a grinding of black pepper.

Lay the salmon fillets over the mushrooms, filling the gaps so each slice will hold some, season, sprinkle with the chopped eggs and herbs, then cover with the other half of the mushrooms and onions. Season and finish the sandwich with the rest of the millet. Wet the edges of the dough, draw them up and fold them over the top – provided the dough tapers rather than thickens towards the edges it should flatten down quite easily, but you may need to cut out the corners before you fold up the ends (these bits of dough can go towards the decoration). Now you will need another pair of hands, if your pie is large, to help you convey it to a greased baking sheet, without it folding or breaking. To decorate your pie, roll out the reserved bit of dough and cut it into leaves or flowers, or whatever. Damp them on one side and lay them gently on the top of the pastry. Brush the whole of the top with beaten egg – your fingers will do – and bake in the oven at 200°C (400°F) mark 6 until it is golden brown.

143

Flammeküche

This is a recipe from Sue Style's book, *A Taste of Alsace*. A sort of northern answer to the pizza. Very simple to make and always a knock–out.

2-3 SERVINGS

FOR THE DOUGH
700 g (1½ lb) strong white flour
1 sachet fast action dried yeast
1 teaspoon salt
2 tablespoons olive oil
1 egg, beaten

FOR THE TOPPING
150 ml (¼ pint) double cream

150 ml (¼ pint) fromage blanc
2 tablespoons olive oil
salt and black pepper
2 onions, finely chopped
225 g (8 oz) smoked streaky bacon,
   de-rinded and cut into tiny strips

Mix the flour, yeast and salt in a bowl, then mix in the oil and egg, gradually adding enough water to make a pliable dough. Knead the dough, then cover with a clean, damp cloth and leave in a warm place to rise for about 45 minutes or until doubled in size.

Knock the dough back and divide it into one or two pieces. Roll or spread each piece into a thin round and place on oiled baking sheets.

Mix together the cream, fromage blanc, oil and seasonings and spread the mixture over the bases. Sprinkle the onions and bacon on top and bake in the oven at 230°C (450°F) mark 8 for about 15 minutes or until golden.

La Crique

4 SERVINGS
450 g (1 lb) potatoes, peeled
salt and black pepper
2 garlic cloves, chopped

1 tablespoon chopped fresh parsley
2 tablespoons olive oil

Grate the potatoes by hand or in a food processor. Place in a bowl, sprinkle with salt and leave for 10 minutes. Squeeze the potato between your hands to extract as much water as possible, then add the garlic, parsley, salt and pepper. Heat the oil in a heavy-based frying pan and put the mixture in all at once, spreading it to fill the bottom of the pan. Cook until golden brown on both sides.

Spicy Chickpeas

This is a delicious 'munchy' with drinks.

450 g (1 lb) chickpeas	1 tablespoon coriander seeds
salt and black pepper	½ teaspoon chilli powder or 1 dried
3 onions, chopped	chilli, de-seeded and chopped
3 tablespoons vegetable oil	1 tablespoon tomato purée
3 garlic cloves, chopped	a bunch of fresh coriander or parsley,
1 tablespoon cumin seeds	chopped

Soak the chickpeas for at least 4 hours or overnight. Drain them and put them in a saucepan. Cover with water, bring to the boil and boil hard for 20 minutes, then turn the heat down and simmer for about 2 hours. (The cooking time will vary according to the chickpeas, but chickpeas never seem to overcook however long you boil them.) When they are nearly ready, salt the water. If you do this when the chickpeas are raw it will toughen them.

In a heavy-based frying pan large enough to take the chickpeas, fry the onions in the oil for a few minutes, then add the garlic. After a minute or two, add the spices and fry for 1 minute, then stir in the tomato purée and cook for 1 minute. Put in the chickpeas, stir round and heat through. Sprinkle with chopped coriander and black pepper before serving.

Green Beans Szechuan-Style

Szechuan food is famously 'hot', spiced with chillies and Szechuan peppercorns, a reddish-brown aromatic with a distinctive flavour obtainable in Chinese stores. This simple treatment of green beans brings out their own flavour, through the pungent accompaniments. It would make a good follow-up to Peking Dumplings (see page 147) served with a little plain rice. I have adapted the recipe from one given by Ken Hom in *The Taste of China*.

6 SERVINGS

450 g (1 lb) fresh green beans	1 tablespoon white wine vinegar or
2 mild green chillies	rice vinegar
1½ tablespoons peanut (groundnut)	2 tablespoons dry sherry (optional)
oil	2 teaspoons sugar
3 garlic cloves, crushed	2 tablespoons water
1 teaspoon salt	1 teaspoon Szechuan peppercorns
1 dried red chilli (optional)	

145

String the beans, if necessary, and snap in two. Cut the green chillies in half, de-seed and slice thinly. Heat the oil in a wok or large frying pan, add the garlic and salt and turn over a high heat for a few seconds. Add the green chillies and stir-fry for about another 10 seconds or until the chilli is softening. If you are using a dried red chilli, de-seed it and crush it finely. Add it to the pan with the beans and all the other ingredients, except the peppercorns. Stir-fry for about 5 minutes or until the beans are just tender. Add a little more water if they look like drying out and catching. Heat the peppercorns in a small saucepan until they release their aroma and are roasted. Crush the peppercorns and sprinkle over the dish before serving.

Ginger-Stuffed Chicken Legs

Transforms sinewy drumsticks into exciting spicy parcels.

6 SERVINGS

2 small onions, finely chopped
5 cm (2 inch) piece of fresh root
   ginger, peeled and finely chopped
1 fresh or dried chilli, de-seeded and
   finely chopped
grated rind of 1 lemon
a generous bunch of fresh parsley or
   coriander, finely chopped

225 g (8 oz) minced pork
soy sauce
black peppercorns, ground
6 chicken legs
2-3 tablespoons vegetable oil

Mix the onions, ginger, chilli, lemon rind and parsley or coriander with the pork, a generous splash of soy sauce and ground peppercorns.

Remove the bones from the drumsticks by turning them inside out and cutting the bones free with a small sharp knife – tear the skin as little as you can but don't worry too much about what happens inside the drumstick. Turn them the right way out again and stuff with the pork mixture. Pull the skin around the re-formed legs and sew up with a large needle and thick thread.

Heat the oil in a flameproof casserole and fry the chicken parcels gently for 5 minutes or until they begin to brown, then transfer to the oven at 180°C (350°F) mark 4 and cook for 25 minutes or until they are well browned and the juices run clear. Serve with rice.

Grilled Aubergines and Sesame Chicken Breasts with Garlic Rice

(6 SERVINGS)

6 chicken breasts, boned
2 tablespoons sesame oil
2 tablespoons sunflower oil
4 garlic cloves, chopped
salt and black pepper

3 large aubergines
125 g (4 oz) sesame seeds
1 teaspoon finely ground sea salt
700 g (1½ lb) long-grain rice

Cut the chicken breasts down the middle into two thin fillets. Mix together the sesame oil, sunflower oil and garlic in a bowl. Add the
chicken, stir to coat, then leave to marinate for 30 minutes.

Remove the chicken pieces from the marinade, reserving the marinade. Sprinkle the chicken pieces with salt and grill them quickly.

Cut the aubergines into slices about 2.5 cm (1 inch) thick. Brush
with some of the reserved chicken marinade, sprinkle with salt and
grill until soft and golden.

Toast the sesame seeds in a dry pan, then stir the sea salt in with them
while they are very hot. Arrange the aubergine and chicken fillets
overlapping alternately on a serving dish and sprinkle with the toasted
sesame seeds and black pepper.

Meanwhile, cook the rice in boiling salted water for about 12
minutes or according to the manufacturer's instructions. Put the remaining chicken marinade in a heavy-based saucepan large enough to
hold the rice. Add a little extra oil if necessary and cook until the garlic
is just golden. Drain the cooked rice and stir it into the garlic oil. Serve
immediately with the chicken and aubergines.

Jiaozi (Peking Dumplings)

As a child reared on northern Chinese cooking, jiaozi were food to
dream about, a birthday treat. I used to watch Lim, our cook, and the
amah gossiping with much cackling laughter as they filled tray after
tray with these savoury dumplings, plump as little goldfish in their
pleated cases of white dough. Fillings vary in detail, but a mixture of
finely chopped pork, prawns and Chinese cabbage, spiked with soy
sauce and aromatic sesame oil, is a constant. Sealed throughout cooking, the concentrated flavour as you munch, is mind-blowing.

147

Reading Ken Hom's book, *The Taste of China*, reminded me that steam-frying jiaozi saves much last-minute flap. This is a treat for a celebration with close friends – crude food, but incomparable. Quantities here yield about six jiaozi each. Serve them piping hot, in bowls, with dipping sauces, and eat with chopsticks. Finish, perhaps, with a thin, clear, quickly made egg drop soup, palate cleansing in true Chinese style.

6-8 SERVINGS

FOR THE JIAOZI DOUGH
350 g (12 oz) strong white flour
about 350 ml (12 fl oz) very hot
*   water*

FOR THE FILLING
275 g (10 oz) Chinese cabbage,
*   finely chopped*
175 g (6 oz) minced pork
175 g (6 oz) prawns, preferably
*   uncooked, peeled and chopped*
6 spring onions, finely chopped
2 garlic cloves, finely chopped

1 tablespoon light soy sauce
1 tablespoon dark soy sauce
1 tablespoon dry sherry (optional)
25 g (1 oz) dried Chinese black
*   mushrooms, soaked in warm*
*   water for 30-60 minutes, then*
*   drained and chopped*
1 tablespoon sesame oil
1 teaspoon salt
a generous grinding of black pepper
4 tablespoons peanut or safflower oil
300 ml (½ pint) hot water

Make the dough first. Sift the flour into a large bowl and pour in the hot water, whisking steadily until the ingredients come together in a ball. The dough should not be sticky, but moist enough to gather up tidily. Transfer to a floured board and knead until smooth and elastic. Return to the bowl and cover with a clean, damp cloth. Set aside.

Combine the filling ingredients in another bowl, mixing thoroughly with your hands, and set aside.

Knead the dough again on a floured board, then shape it into a long sausage about 2.5-4 cm (1-1½ inches) in diameter. Cut off a slice about 2 cm (¾ inch) wide, flatten it with the palm of your hand, then roll it out thinly with a floured rolling pin to make a circle about 9 cm (3½ inches) across. Continue rolling slices until you have used up all the dough, covering the rounds with a clean, damp cloth meanwhile.

To shape and fill the jiaozi, pinch three or four pleats in one side of each dough circle to create a concave shape. Pop 2 teaspoons of the filling into each hollow, fold the two sides together and pinch to close (a trace of water along the join can help), making a plump little crescent shape. Lay these on a lightly floured tray, cover with a clean, damp cloth and set aside until you have filled all the jiaozi.

To steam-fry the jiaozi, heat the oil in a wok or large frying pan,

148

then pack the jiaozi in closely in a single layer. Cook over a moderate heat until the bases of the jiaozi are browned. Pour over the hot water, cover and cook over a high heat for 2 minutes. Lower the heat to a simmer and continue to cook, still covered, for another 8-10 minutes or until most of the cooking water has been absorbed. Uncover and continue cooking until the pan is dry and sizzling and the dumplings are crisp and golden brown on the bottom. Serve at once with the following dipping sauces; either in larger communal bowls or little individual bowls: dark soy sauce; light soy sauce with a dash of white wine vinegar; chilli bean sauce.

N O T E : *Unless you have two pans on the go, the jiaozi will need preparing in relays, but compared with the boiling procedure, the involvement at this stage is minimal.*

Choucroute à l'Alsacienne

This recipe is indebted to Sue Style's *A Taste of Alsace*, though I have pruned it a little to bring it within pauper budgets. This is a fine dish for a winter party, a peasant feast of pungent flavours, particularly easy to prepare and the kind of big hotpot that can be left to cook longer without spoiling if you turn the oven down a notch.

6-8 SERVINGS

1.5 kg (3 lb) sauerkraut, canned, bottled or sold in plastic packs	1 smoked sausage ring
	1 bay leaf
15 g (½ oz) butter, lard or bacon fat	1 teaspoon juniper berries
2 onions, chopped	1 teaspoon coriander seeds
2 garlic cloves, crushed	2 cloves
450 g (1 lb) belly of pork in one piece, rubbed with salt and left overnight	6 peppercorns
	600 ml (1 pint) dry white wine
	600 ml (1 pint) stock or water
400 g (14 oz) smoked bacon in one piece	1.5 kg (3 lb) large potatoes
	6-8 canned frankfurters

Tip the sauerkraut (choucroute) into cold water and wash well, changing the water once or twice. Drain, then squeeze out the moisture. Melt the fat in a large flameproof casserole and soften the onions and garlic over a low heat. Wipe the belly of pork free of salt. Lay half the choucroute on the bottom of the pan, add the bacon, pork belly and smoked sausage ring on top, scatter the herbs and spices over, cover with the remaining choucroute, pour over the wine and stock or

water, and bring to a gentle simmer. Cover, transfer to the oven and
cook at 180°C (350°F) mark 4 for 2 hours. Check that the liquid level is
okay, topping up with water if necessary.

Meanwhile, steam the potatoes briefly in their skins, then peel and
cut into chunks. Prick the frankfurters, and gently heat through, but
do not boil or they will burst.

Dish up on your biggest platter thus: a mound of choucroute in the
centre, potatoes at each end, and sliced meats, sausage and frankfurters
spread appetisingly on top. Serve with mustard.

Home-made Venison Sausages

A home-made sausage, lets face it, has real style. Made with venison,
this is dinner party food, a bother to make but on the other hand bril-
liantly easy to cook. Venison is too lean to make a juicy sausage, so the
fatty pork makes up for this deficiency as well as reducing the cost.
Serve with one of the mixed vegetable purées, or lentils, braised red
cabbage, and Onion Compote (see opposite), or Cumberland sauce.

4-5 SERVINGS
1 kg (2 lb) belly of pork
1 kg (2 lb) venison off the bone
225 g (8 oz) hard back pork fat
1 tablespoon coriander seeds
6 allspice berries
6 cloves
1 tablespoon black peppercorns
3 garlic cloves, crushed
2 tablespoons salt
1 glass of red wine or port
pig casings (see Note)

Cut the rind and rib bones from the belly of pork and put it through the
mincer with the venison. Cut the pork back fat into tiny cubes and mix
these with the meat. Pound the spices to a coarse powder in a mortar,
and mix into the minced meat with your hands, together with the
garlic and salt. Pour over the wine or port. Mix again, then leave to
stand for about 2 hours. Stuff the sausage casings to make short, fat
links. Leave in a cool place for 24 hours to develop the flavours before
cooking.

NOTE: *Some family butchers stock animal casings, or you can order them
by post. (One good supplier is Smithfield Casings, West Burrowfield,
Welwyn Garden City, Herts AL7 4TW. Tel: 0707 328 557.) Packed in salt
in a jar, they will keep for ages in the fridge. Soak in water before use.*

Onion Compote

This is a delectable way to make use of little pickling onions or shallots, and is no trouble once you have peeled the onions. Serve with cold meat, or sausages, or alone with dark rye bread as an original starter.

4 SERVINGS

450-700 g (1-1½ lb) pickling onions or shallots

200 ml (7 fl oz) water

1 tablespoon wine vinegar

3 tablespoons olive oil

1 tablespoon brown sugar or honey

2 tablespoons tomato purée

3 tablespoons raisins, sultanas or currants

a sprig of fresh thyme, a bay leaf, and a sprig of fresh rosemary, tied together

salt and pepper

To peel the onions or shallots, blanch them in a large saucepan of boiling water for about 10 seconds, then drain them and rinse under cold running water. Trim off both ends and slip off the skins.

Put the onions or shallots in a large heavy-based saucepan with the remaining ingredients. Bring to the boil, then turn the heat right down and simmer gently, half-covered, for 30–45 minutes or until the onions or shallots are tender and most of the liquid has evaporated. Check from time to time that the liquid is not catching and burning – always a danger with a mixture that includes sugar or honey. Add a splash more water if this looks likely. Remove the herbs and season with salt and pepper. Serve warm or cold.

Boiled Salt Silverside

I am indebted to Arabella Boxer's *English Food* for this traditional British dish. It costs less per pound than a roasting cut and I find it makes an impressive dinner party dish, its fine red colour set off by boiled potatoes and carrots.

6-8 SERVINGS

a rolled cut of salt silverside, weighing 1.4-1.6 kg (3-3½ lb)

3 carrots

2 onions, each studded with two cloves

1 celery stick

1 tablespoon black peppercorns

1 bay leaf

Wash the rolled beef, then put it in a heavy-based saucepan large enough to take the beef and vegetables. Cover with cold water to about 2.5 cm (1 inch) above the beef. Bring very slowly to the boil, skimming off any froth. When boiling, add the carrots, onions, celery, peppercorns and bay leaf. Turn the heat down and cook, partly covered, for 2 hours, topping up with hot water if the liquid drops below the beef.

If eating hot, remove to a warmed serving dish, cutting off any string. Serve surrounded by separately cooked carrots, and boiled potatoes. If the broth is not too salty, stir a little mild mustard into a gravyboatful and pass this round, to moisten the beef.

For eating cold, let the beef cool in its liquid. This keeps it juicy. Don't be put off by the greyish exterior of the silverside; once cut, the inside is an almost garnet red.

Bollito Misto

8-10 SERVINGS

2 celery sticks, cut into short
  lengths
2 carrots, roughly chopped
1 onion, roughly chopped
900 g (2 lb) piece of beef brisket
salt
1 chicken

FOR THE SAUCE
a large bunch of fresh parsley

1 garlic clove
1 tablespoon capers, drained
6 anchovy fillets, drained
½ teaspoon mustard
½ teaspoon wine vinegar
175 ml (6 fl oz) olive oil
a pinch of salt (if needed)

Put the celery, carrots and onion in a very large saucepan or flameproof casserole with enough water to cover the meat and chicken when they are put in. Bring to the boil, then put in the piece of brisket. Return the water to the boil and skim off any scum that comes to the top. Add a little salt, put the lid on so that it almost covers the pan, and turn the heat down so that the water just simmers. Let the beef simmer for 2 hours on its own, then put in the whole chicken and continue simmering for a further 1 hour.

To make the sauce, chop the parsley, garlic and capers together finely. Mash the anchovy fillets and mix all the ingredients together, seasoning with more vinegar or a pinch of salt, if necessary.

When the meat and chicken are cooked, remove them from the hot stock and cut slices off them to serve. Return the leftover meat and chicken to the hot stock. Serve the slices of meat with just a very little of the stock, some plain boiled potatoes and a generous tablespoon of the green sauce. The stock and whatever meat is left will provide an excellent soup for the next day.

Chinese Spiced Beef

For this dish, you must have star anise, a pretty star-shaped spice, which can be bought cheaply at Chinese food stores and some supermarkets. It gives the meat an absolutely unique and delicious taste and aroma. For the rest, it is a gratifyingly easy recipe to prepare, the kind you can leave quietly cooking while you talk to your guests.

8 SERVINGS

900 g (2 lb) shin of beef in one piece	2 garlic cloves
2 tablespoons oil	1 star anise
1 tablespoon soy sauce	1 tablespoon sugar
2 teaspoons wine or wine vinegar	buttered noodles, to serve
pepper	

If the meat is ragged-looking, tie it up neatly with string. Heat the oil in a frying pan, add the meat and cook until browned all over. Add the soy sauce, wine or vinegar, pepper, garlic cloves (whole), and 4 tablespoons water, and simmer slowly, covered, for 10 minutes. Add the star anise. Put the pan on an asbestos mat, cover, and cook very slowly for 1 hour. Add the sugar, turn the meat over, re-cover and simmer for another hour.

To serve, boil up a lot of egg noodles in salted water. Stir a little butter and soy sauce into them, and pile up in one large dish. Take the meat out of the pan, cut the string and slice on to a warmed plate. Pour over the juices from the pan. Serve the meat and juice with the buttered noodles.

If you must serve a vegetable, it should be a Chinese-style vegetable dish – stir-fried cabbage or beat sprouts would be excellent.

Guinea Fowl and Lentils

The guinea fowl is a terrific bird, far more festive and deliciously gamey than chicken. It feeds more people than any game bird and usually costs much less (about the same as free-range chicken). Serve it with a dish of lentils and some salad and it will be a feast.

8 SERVINGS

2 guinea fowl

10-12 garlic cloves

175 g (6 oz) butter

12 shallots, skinned (optional)

2 sprigs of fresh rosemary

olive oil

salt and (preferably coarse) black pepper

800 g (1¾ lb) green (Puy) or brown lentils

250 ml (8 fl oz) hot water

grated rind of 1 lemon (optional)

Finish plucking the guinea fowl – butchers and supermarkets often leave a few feathers in so you can be sure what you're getting. Crush four or five garlic cloves and put them with a generous knob of butter into each bird. Oil a casserole or earthenware baking dish and put the shallots on the bottom, then the rosemary sprigs on top of the shallots. Rub the guinea fowl with oil and salt and lay them on their sides on the shallots and rosemary. Cook them in the oven at 220°C (425°F) mark 7 for 20 minutes, then turn them on to their other side for a further 20 minutes, basting every so often with the butter that runs from them. Finish them breast-up so that this browns.

Meanwhile, heat the remaining butter and 4 tablespoons oil in a large sauté pan and put in the remaining whole garlic cloves. Stir for a minute, then put in the lentils. Turn the lentils about in the oil for 1-2 minutes, then pour over the hot water. Let it sizzle, then cover the lentils with hot water and keep them over a fairly robust heat, topping up with water if you need to, until they are ready. Don't stir them too much or they will get knocked about and become a bit mushy. When they are ready, but still firmish, season with salt to taste and plenty of black pepper and just before you bring them to the table, a splash of good olive oil and lemon rind if you are using it.

Dorset Rabbit Pie

Rabbit can sometimes be dry – this is an old-fashioned way of sealing in their moisture and flavour. Eat it on its own (perhaps after a first course of salad) or with some simply cooked broad beans.

6 SERVINGS

2 rabbits

seasoned flour

450 g (1 lb) fresh breadcrumbs

8 large onions, very finely chopped

grated rind of 1 lemon

salt and pepper

a small bunch of fresh sage, finely cut

2 eggs

2 tablespoons milk

5 rashers of unsmoked streaky bacon, de-rinded

Joint the rabbits, dust them with seasoned flour, and put them in a straight-sided casserole. Mix the breadcrumbs, onion, lemon rind, salt and pepper and the sage leaves together and bind with the eggs and milk. Cover the rabbit with the rashers of bacon and lay the 'stuffing' over the top. Cook in the oven at 200°C (400°F) mark 6 for 2 hours, covering it with greaseproof paper if it seems to be browning too soon.

Tuscan Rabbit with Prunes

Serve with plenty of pappardelle and a green salad.

8 SERVINGS

2 rabbits	1 glass of Marsala
boiling tea	6 garlic cloves, chopped
about 12 prunes	1 sprig of fresh thyme or marjoram
olive oil	salt and pepper
1 glass of red wine	

Joint the rabbits, cutting the saddles into two pieces so that more people can get the best bits. Pour boiling tea on to the prunes and leave for 15 minutes. Drain the prunes and put them with the rabbit in a marinade of a glass each of olive oil, wine and Marsala. Cover and leave for at least 1 hour or the whole day (if it's for supper) in the fridge.

In a heavy flameproof casserole, heat 2 tablespoons olive oil and brown the rabbit pieces. Add the garlic with the herbs to the rabbit, cook for a scant minute, then pour over the reserved marinade and the prunes. Season with a little salt and plenty of black pepper, put the lid on tightly and cook in the oven at 180°C (350°F) mark 4 for at least 2 hours. You may cook it harder for a shorter time but the gentle simmering makes for the richest flavour. Serve with egg pappardelle or wide noodles.

'Peking' Breast of Lamb with Pancakes and Slivered Spring Onions

This is the pauper's version of a famous Chinese feast dish. Breast of lamb is a very cheap cut which, like duck, is fatty and flavoursome, and during long slow cooking in a honey glaze will become crispy on the outside with rich shreds of meat on the inside. You can make the pancakes yourself, following the recipe below or, if you can get to a Chinese supermarket, buy them ready-made. There's no pretending it isn't time-consuming making the pancakes, but it should make you pretty proud of yourself!

1 breast of lamb	**FOR THE PANCAKES**
salt	*175 g (6 oz) plain flour*
4 tablespoons honey	*a pinch of salt*
2 bunches of spring onions, cut into	*100 ml (4 fl oz) boiling water*
5-7.5 cm (2-3 inch) slivers	*sesame oil*
Hoisin sauce (see Note), to serve	

Immerse the lamb in boiling water for 3 minutes, then drain it, pat it dry with absorbent kitchen paper and place it on a rack to dry. Rub it with salt. Dilute the honey with enough boiling water to make it liquid and brush it on to the lamb until it is completely saturated. Leave it on the rack to dry out again overnight or for as long as possible.

Place the breast of lamb on a rack over a roasting tin and cook in the oven at 170–180°C (325–350°F) mark 3–4 for 1 hour or until it is brown and crisp. With a sharp knife and fork, cut the lamb off the bone and serve with a heap of steamed pancakes, a plate of slivered spring onions and a bowl of Hoisin sauce. Each diner should spread his pancake with some of the sauce, a piece or two of the spring onion and some of the sweet crispy meat.

To make the pancakes, sift together the flour and salt in a deep bowl, pour on the boiling water and mix. The mixture will seem rather dry to begin with, but should end up as a dryish dough. Since flours vary in absorbency, you may need more boiling water, but use it sparingly.

Knead the dough until it stretches fairly elastically, then put it on a floured board and pat with a rolling pin or milk bottle, until it is a long oblong roll about 2 cm (¾ inch) thick. Cut this across into chunks 4 cm (1½ inches) wide, and divide these into 4 cm (1½ inch) squares. Take two squares, flatten each slightly with the rolling pin, dip a finger into a saucer of oil and smear it over one side of one square. Then clap the other square on top, like a little sandwich, and roll them both out together until very thin and roughly circular.

Put a few drops of oil in a frying pan and spread it over the base of the pan with greaseproof paper – it must be greaseproof or it will absorb the oil. When the oil is moderately hot, put in the pancake and leave for a minute until it is light brown or a deep cream colour underneath. (If black spots appear your pan may be too hot, or the heat may be uneven.) Turn the pancake over and cook the other side the same way. The pan may need re-oiling before starting the next pancake.

As the pancakes are cooked, keep them warm by standing them on a saucer in a colander which is resting on the bottom of a large pan with a little water simmering in the bottom. This keeps them warm without drying them out.

Repeat the process, oiling the pan as needed, until all the pancakes are cooked. Serve with the lamb, Hoisin sauce and spring onions.

N O T E : *If you cannot get Hoisin sauce, use soy sauce with a little sugar added.*

Chicken Maryland

What sets Chicken Maryland apart, I think, is the trimmings – corn fritters and fried bananas. Sweet potatoes, or yams, which can be bought in some large markets, particularly in London, would be an authentic accompaniment.

4 SERVINGS

1 young chicken, cut into 4 joints, or 4 chicken portions	FOR THE TRIMMINGS
1 tablespoon plain flour, seasoned with salt, pepper and paprika	*about 225 g (8 oz) canned corn kernels, or 2 fresh or frozen corn cobs*
1 egg, beaten	*2 eggs, separated*
dry breadcrumbs	*salt and pepper*
15 g (½ oz) butter	*1 teaspoon baking powder*
2 tablespoons vegetable oil	*125-150 g (4-5 oz) soft white breadcrumbs*
a little soured cream	*butter, for frying*
watercress, to garnish	*4-8 bananas*

To prepare the chicken, put the seasoned flour in a polythene bag with the chicken pieces, and shake until well coated. Dip the chicken pieces in beaten egg and roll in breadcrumbs until covered. Heat the butter and oil in a pan large enough to take all the chicken, and fry the pieces gently, over a moderate heat for 30–45 minutes or until well done all over, turning occasionally. Add a little soured cream to the juices in the pan a few minutes before serving, scraping up the debris with a wooden spoon, and leave to bubble gently.

Meanwhile, in a second frying pan, make the corn fritters. For these, you must drain the corn, if canned, or boil it for about 10 minutes and scrape it off the cobs, if fresh or frozen. Beat the egg yolks and add to the corn. Season with salt and pepper. Beat the egg whites until stiff and fold in. Add the baking powder, and enough breadcrumbs to make the mixture thick and dry enough to handle. Shape into little cakes. Melt some butter in a large frying pan and fry the corn fritters until brown on both sides. Put them in a dish and keep them warm in the oven at 130°C (250°F) mark ½. Peel the bananas, slice them lengthways and fry them gently in butter until soft.

If the corn fritters seem like too much of a performance, you could serve the kernels just as they are, with a little butter or soured cream stirred in. But don't skip the fried bananas.

Serve the chicken on a long plate, garnished with watercress and the fried bananas. Serve the corn separately. Baked sweet potatoes, with butter, or plain baked potatoes, would be a nice easy accompaniment.

Steak and Kidney Pudding

This is an excellent dish with which to impress. It is actually rather easy to make, but doesn't look it. The quantities given make a large pudding – it might be better to try a half-size pudding first.

6-8 SERVINGS

3-4 sheep's kidneys or 450 g (1 lb) ox kidney	seasoned flour
900 g (2 lb) stewing steak or shin of beef	225 g (8 oz) plain flour
	salt and pepper
	125 g (4 oz) shredded beef suet

Clean the kidneys well, removing all gristle and the cores. Skin them and chop them into small pieces. Cut the beef into 2.5 cm (1 inch) cubes and roll them in seasoned flour.

To make the suetcrust pastry, sift together the flour and a pinch of salt. Add the suet and stir in 6-8 tablespoons water, enough to make a stiff dough. Roll this out and use to line a pudding basin, keeping about a third of the pastry to cover the top with. Put in the beef pieces and kidney, and add enough water to come within 2.5 cm (1 inch) of the top. Season with salt and pepper, then put on the pastry lid. Crimp the edges together and press them down over the rim of the bowl. Place a piece of foil over the top, tied with string round the ridge at the top of the basin.

Put 5 cm (2 inches) of water in the bottom of a large saucepan with a tight-fitting lid. If possible, stand something on the bottom to rest the bowl on – an inverted saucer would do. Put the pudding in when the water boils. Cover the pan tightly and simmer steadily for 3-4 hours. About 30 minutes before the meal, take the pudding out, remove the foil cap, and put the pudding in the oven at 190°C (375°F) mark 5 to brown the top. (This part is not essential, but it does improve the appearance.)

If the pan lid is not tight fitting you will have to check from time to time to see if the water has boiled away. It will almost certainly need replenishing with more *boiling* water.

With a classic dish like this, serve Brussels sprouts or cabbage, boiled for 5 minutes or so, well drained and braised in a little butter.

Lamb Tagine with Couscous

6-8 SERVINGS

200 g (7 oz) prunes	*1 tablespoon ground coriander*
900 g (2 lb) lamb with some fat, e.g.	*5 cm (2 inch) cinnamon stick, or*
shoulder, boned	*1 teaspoon ground cinnamon*
vegetable or olive oil	*1 teaspoon ground turmeric*
2 large onions, chopped	*2 cooking apples*
5 garlic cloves, chopped	*800 g (1¾ lb) couscous*
1 teaspoon ground ginger	*salt*

Soak the prunes overnight. Cut the lamb into roughly 2.5 cm (1 inch) cubes, removing any skin, bone and gristle. Heat some oil in a deep flameproof casserole, add the onion, garlic and spices and heat gently until 'the smell comes out', as they say. (This may sound vague, but the experience is unambiguous.) Add the lamb, and toss in the oil for 2-3 minutes just to seal the meat without browning it. Pour over enough hot water to cover, and put on the lid. Bring to the boil, then lower the heat and simmer gently (or cook in the oven at 170°C/325°F/ mark 3) for about 2 hours or until the meat is tender and the liquid has thickened.

Drain the prunes and peel, core and quarter the apples. Add both to the stew and simmer, uncovered, for another 20-30 minutes or until the fruit is soft, and the liquid slightly reduced.

To make couscous in an authentic manner is a bit of a palaver, but simple enough once the principle of the cold water wetting and swelling, followed by steaming, is grasped. For best results, this needs to be done twice, the second time steaming the couscous over the simmering tagine.

First, spread the couscous in a shallow dish and moisten with cold water. Leave for a few minutes for the grains to swell, breaking up lumps with your fingers. Transfer the couscous to a colander and set it over a pan of boiling water. The water must not touch the couscous,

159

but on the other hand you need to channel the steam through the grain, so wrap a tea-towel round the join between colander and pan. Steam for 30 minutes, uncovered.

Turn the couscous into a dish again, sprinkle generously with more cold water, and rake with your fingers to aerate further. Add a very little oil and salt to make the swollen grains glisten. Return the couscous to the colander and set it over the simmering tagine, wrapping a cloth around the join as before. The fragrant steam will give the couscous more flavour. Steam for 30 minutes, then serve the couscous heaped into a golden cone on a hot platter, with the tagine passed round for everyone to help themselves.

N O T E : *I should add that tagine is not strictly the correct accompaniment to a classic couscous, but I find they make a splendidly tasty and festive party combination. Serve harissa in small bowls. This is the fiery condiment that gives a pleasurable jolt to many Middle Eastern dishes. To make your own, soak 25 g (1 oz) dried red chillies in hot water for 1 hour. Drain, then pound to a paste in a mortar with 1 large garlic clove and a little salt. Spoon this into a tiny jar, cover the harissa with a film of olive oil, and the jar with cling film, and keep in a cool place. It is customary to add some of this to the cooking juices for passing round like a 'hot' gravy.*

If, on the other hand, couscous seems altogether too much sweat, substitute Burghul with Raisins and Nuts (see page 65) instead, or even Hot Savoury Rice (see page 59) with some gravy stirred in at the last minute.

Baked Gammon

Gammon, baked with a glistening brown crust of molasses, mustard and vinegar, studded with cloves and surrounded by spicy fruit, is one meat I could happily eat for weeks on end.

Cuts of cheaper boiling bacon, sold in plastic packs, can be cooked in the same way. These can be extra salty. To deal with this, place the meat in a large saucepan, cover with water and bring slowly to the boil. Throw away the water and repeat with fresh water.

4-6 SERVINGS

1 small corner of gammon, weighing about 1.1-1.4 kg (2½-3 lb)	1 bay leaf
	vinegar
a few dried apricots	cloves
1 onion, studded with 2 cloves	molasses or brown sugar
1 carrot	mustard

Soak the gammon and dried apricots overnight in cold water. Drain the meat and put it in a saucepan of fresh cold water with the onion, carrot and bay leaf. Bring very slowly to the boil over a low heat. Keep the water only faintly simmering, and cook for roughly 20 minutes per 450 g (1 lb), stopping a little short of the full time allowance, as the joint will be finished off in the oven. If you don't want to bake it straight away, leave the meat to cool in the cooking water – this keeps it moist and tender.

While the gammon is cooking, drain the apricots and cook in a little water with 1 tablespoon vinegar and a clove or two. Drain when soft and reserve the water.

To bake the gammon, first remove it from the water and strip off the rind with a sharp knife, leaving most of the fat. (This part does not apply to boiling bacon cuts.) Score a lattice pattern on the fat with the point of a knife and stick a clove into the middle of each little pane of fat. Mix some molasses or brown sugar, vinegar and mustard together – the amount varies with the size of your joint, but the proportions are roughly 1 tablespoon molasses to 2 teaspoons vinegar and 1 teaspoon mustard.

Put the gammon in a roasting tin and spoon the mixture over it, scooping it out of the tin and repeating the process until the fat is brown and sticky. Surround the meat with apricots and bake in the oven at 180°C (350°F) mark 4 for about 30 minutes, basting once or twice with the juices in the pan, supplemented with a little apricot water if necessary.

To serve, transfer the joint to a large plate, with the apricots all around. Dilute the juice left in the roasting tin with a little more apricot water, heat and serve as gravy.

I think ham and gammon need only the plainest accompaniments – baked jacket potatoes, a dish of buttered peas, or a faintly bitter salad with curly endive, and lots of freshly made mustard.

 ## Hand of Pork Candied Chinese-Style

At the time of going to press, the butcher was selling hands of pork for 40p a pound, one of the cheapest things in his window. In this recipe, the highly flavoured pork can be served as part of a Chinese meal with other vegetable and rice dishes – a way of making this small joint satisfy a party.

6-10 SERVINGS

1 hand of pork	*3 tablespoons dry sherry*
10 cm (4 inch) piece of fresh root	*25 g (1 oz) brown sugar*
ginger, peeled and thickly sliced	*3 spring onions, halved lengthways*
6 tablespoons thick soy sauce	

Put the pork in a heavy-based saucepan and cover with cold water. Bring to the boil and boil, uncovered, for 5 minutes. Pour off the water and scum, then return the pork to the pan, skin side down (Yan Kit recommends resting it on a bamboo mat if possible, to prevent the pork sticking to the bottom). Add the ginger, spring onions, soy sauce, sherry, sugar and about 1.1 litres (2 pints) water. Bring to the boil, then put on the lid and reduce the heat. Leave to simmer for 1 hour, occasionally loosing the joint from the bottom of the pan.

After the first hour, turn the joint over and put more water in, if necessary, to make sure it comes one third of the way up the pork. Replace the lid and continue to simmer gently for a further hour, again moving the joint about occasionally to prevent it sticking.

Remove the lid and turn the heat up a little so the liquid boils and reduces. Baste the joint with the sauce as it thickens. When you are satisfied with the texture of the sauce, discard the ginger and spring onions and pour the sauce over the steaming pork.

 ## Steamed Lemon Mousse

This is a lovely pudding, fragrant and delicate – English cooking at its most harmonious. It has a summery feel about it, but as lemons are available all year round you could equally well serve it as a refreshing sequel to a heavy winter meal.

4 SERVINGS

6 eggs, separated	*150 g (5 oz) granulated sugar*
150 g (5 oz) butter	*grated rind and juice of 1 lemon*

Put the egg yolks, butter, sugar, lemon juice and grated lemon rind in the top of a double saucepan or in a heatproof bowl over barely simmering water. Stir with a wooden spoon until the custard thickens. It must not boil, or the eggs will scramble. The secret is to keep the water underneath only just simmering, and to stir until the mixture reaches custard thickness, and no longer. Remove from the heat and continue to stir until cold (this takes less time than you would expect – a few minutes).

Stiffly whisk the egg whites and fold them into the mixture. Turn into a buttered or oiled (vegetable oil, not olive oil, which has too pronounced a taste) pudding basin, then cover the basin with a plate or a cap of foil. Stand the basin in a saucepan with about 2.5 cm (1 inch) of gently boiling water in the bottom. Cover the pan itself and steam for about 1 hour or until the mousse if firm.

Leave to cool, then turn out on to a dish.

 # Orange Jelly

This makes the most delicious jelly – soft and wobbly, with an incomparably fresh flavour. Blood oranges are especially good in this recipe, when available.

4 SERVINGS

9 large oranges	15 g (½ oz) powdered gelatine
1 lemon	2 tablespoons water
125 g (4 oz) caster sugar	

Thinly peel the rind from one orange and half the lemon.

Put the sugar in a small saucepan with 4 tablespoons water and heat gently, stirring occasionally, until the sugar dissolves. Bring to the boil and boil for 5–10 minutes to form a syrup. Pour on to the orange and lemon rind while still boiling.

Squeeze the juice from all the oranges, and the lemon, and strain through a nylon sieve. Put 2 tablespoons water in a cup and sprinkle the gelatine on top. Leave to soften for 5 minutes, then stand the cup in a saucepan of gently simmering water and heat until the gelatine has dissolved. Strain the syrup and add to the fruit juices with the dissolved gelatine. Pour into a bowl or separate glasses and leave until set.

Meringues and Cream

Home-made meringues have nothing in common with the commercial variety, which explode into brittle shards when you take an incautious bite. The home-made meringue is faintly crisp outside, tacky within and the palest honey colour. Two meringues per person, sandwiched with whipped cream and topped with a trickle of melted chocolate, are a delectable dessert, which is simple to make.

One egg white gives you four smallish meringues. But this is such a popular pudding it is best to make a few over.

4 SERVINGS

4 egg whites	300 ml (½ pint) whipping cream
8 heaped tablespoons caster sugar	225 g (8 oz) plain chocolate
a few drops of vanilla flavouring	

To make the meringues, whisk the egg whites until they stand in peaks. Add the caster sugar a little at a time, whisking constantly until the mixture is smooth and thick. Add a few drops of vanilla flavouring and whisk briefly. Drop the mixture in spoonfuls on to a greased baking sheet, and cook in the oven at 110°C (225°F) mark ¼ until faintly tinged with colour. If you are not in a hurry, it is a good idea to stand the meringues in a draught for a while to dry off *before* putting them in the oven.

To make the filling, whip the cream until it is fluffy. You can sweeten it, but I find the plain cream contrasts well with the sweet meringue. Sandwich the meringues together with the cream. Melt the chocolate in a little water in a low oven, just before serving. Stir it until smooth, and make a little doodle over each meringue sandwich.

N O T E : *Meringues are the ideal way to use up leftover egg whites.*

Mont Blanc

A sumptuous pudding, this, and like so many of the best inventions, simplicity itself – a mound of sieved, sweetened chestnut with a cap of whipped cream. The only problem is peeling your chestnuts. Easier to do while they are piping hot and you are wearing rubber gloves.

4 SERVINGS

450 g (1 lb) fresh chestnuts	whipping cream
a little milk	grated chocolate, to decorate
vanilla sugar or sugar and vanilla	(optional)
flavouring	

Score the chestnuts crosswise across the top and drop them into boiling water. Boil for about 8 minutes, then take out a few chestnuts at a time and remove the outer shell and inner brown skin.

When you have peeled the chestnuts, put them in a saucepan with a little milk sweetened with vanilla sugar (or sugar and vanilla flavouring), and stew for 20–30 minutes or until they are soft. Drain the chestnuts and press them through a sieve, or small colander, so that the chestnut drops like short lengths of vermicelli on to a serving dish.

164

Don't press this into shape, but hollow out the top. Whip the cream until stiff with a little caster sugar and a drop of vanilla flavouring. Spoon it into the hollow on top of the chestnut and sprinkle with grated chocolate, if using.

Sussex Puddle

For this pudding you will need a large (about 1.4 litre/2½ pint) pudding basin and a saucepan big enough to hold it – worthwhile investments if you want steamed puddings in your life (see the other recipes on pages 74 and 158).

6-8 SERVINGS

1 large lemon
225 g (8 oz) self-raising flour
125 g (4 oz) shredded suet
about 150 ml (¼ pint) milk and
    water mixed

125 g (4 oz) slightly salted butter,
    cut into pieces
125 g (4 oz) soft brown sugar

Scrub the lemon to remove any sprays or waxes and prick it all over with a fork. Mix the flour and suet together and gradually add the milk and water until you have a firm dough.

Put the dough on a lightly floured surface and roll it out to a large circle. Cut out a quarter of the cirle for the lid of the pudding, and use the remainder to line a buttered 1.4 litre (2½ pint) pudding basin. Put in half the butter, half the sugar, and the lemon. Put the rest of the butter and sugar on top. Roll out the last quarter of the suet to make a lid, wet the edges and press it on, with a large piece of foil, pleating it to allow for swelling. Tie it round the rim with string.

Lower the basin into a large pan of boiling water so that the water comes at least halfway up the basin. Cover and leave to simmer for 3-4 hours, replenishing with boiling water as necessary.

After steaming, remove the pudding from the saucepan and take off the foil. Bake in the oven at 180°C (350°F) mark 4 for about 20 minutes or until the suet is browned. To serve, loosen the pudding from the basin with a palette knife and turn it out on to a plate.

Dur Mou

This old French family recipe starts with a basic chocolate mousse mixture made with lots of eggs, and ends up with something between a soufflé and a squidgy cake. You then sandwich a layer of the chocolate mousse between two layers of the *dur mou* for an unbelievable, wickedly rich result.

6 SERVINGS

300 g (10 oz) plain chocolate　　　*9 egg yolks*
225 g (8 oz) unsalted butter　　　*a pinch of salt*
225 g (8 oz) sugar　　　*5 egg whites*

Preheat the oven to 150°C (300°F) mark 2. In a bowl placed over a pan of simmering water, melt the chocolate with the butter. Beat the sugar with the egg yolks until smooth. Mix this with the chocolate away from the heat, adding it gradually.

Beat the egg whites in a clean bowl with a tiny pinch of salt until stiff. Fold into the chocolate mixture gently but thoroughly. Have ready two greased 18 cm (7 inch) cake tins. Divide about two-thirds of the cake mixture between the pans and bake in the oven for 1 hour. Meanwhile, keep the remaining chocolate cake mixture/mousse in the fridge.

Let the cakes cool. Spoon the mousse over the cake base and sandwich the two halves together. Eat warm or cold.

Ginger Ice Cream

This is by no means a thrifty recipe except that nobody ought to eat very much of it. Make Almond Biscuits (see opposite) to go with it.

8 SERVINGS

250 ml (8 fl oz) full cream milk　　　*250 ml (8 fl oz) whipping cream*
1 whole egg plus 2 egg yolks　　　*5-6 nuggets of preserved stem ginger,*
3 tablespoons syrup from the bottle of　　　*finely chopped*
*　preserved stem ginger*　　　*2 tablespoons soft brown sugar*

Bring the milk to the boil and pour it very slowly on to the egg and egg yolks, beating hard all the time. Return to the pan and stir over a very low heat until the custard thickens. The moment it is thick enough to coat the back of a wooden spoon, put the base of the pan in a bowl of iced water and stir the ginger syrup into the custard. Pour the custard into a freezerproof container and freeze for 30–40 minutes or until the custard has set solid round the edges.

Whip the cream until it is stiff. Turn the frozen custard into a bowl, stir it up well and quickly stir in the ginger pieces and whipped cream. Taste and add sugar cautiously. Return to the freezer and freeze for

1 hour, then give it another gentle stir, so that the ginger pieces do not sink to the bottom. Freeze until hard.

NOTE: *It is not vital to use the exact quantities of preserved ginger and syrup; the contents of a small jar will do.*

Almond Biscuits

Another good recipe for using up egg whites.

MAKES 6

2 egg whites
a pinch of salt
50 g (2 oz) caster sugar
2 teaspoons flour, sifted

grated rind of ½ lemon
a pinch of ground cinnamon
50 g (2 oz) ground almonds

Whisk the egg whites, adding the salt halfway, until it forms soft peaks. Gradually add the sugar and continue to whisk until stiff. Gently fold in the flour, lemon rind, cinnamon and almonds. Line a baking sheet with greaseproof or rice paper. Drop tablespoons of the mixture on to it and bake in the oven at 150°C (300°F) mark 2 for about 20 minutes or until the little biscuits are golden brown.

Private Enterprise

Most of the recipes in this chapter are for what might be called extras, things which are not essential, but nice to have. Jams, marmalade, sauces and relishes, breads, cakes and biscuits. This type of cooking is fun to do when you are in the right mood. You save some money too, but the real point of home-made items like these is that they taste so much nicer than anything you could buy at a comparable price. They are a luxury paupers can afford.

Many of these recipes can be made equally well by people living in the town or country. But I have included some recipes especially for country-dwellers, because this is where private enterprise really does pay off. Without going to the lengths of buying a gun or fishing tackle, you can still supplement your eating, free, if you know where to look (ask a sympathetic local), and what to look for – a little research in the public library may help here. Quite a few good things grow wild: blackberries, of course, sloes and elderberries. Dandelion leaves for salads (the French actually grow them for the purpose), wild sorrel, highly pungent wild garlic, young nettle shoots for soup. Mushrooms take some tracking down, but they can still be found in suitable spots (hayfields where horses have been pastured are supposed to be ideal) if you get there before other people. This is one subject you must learn up though. Death caps, which look deceptively like edible mush-rooms, are deadly. Safest thing is to get some knowledgeable country-man to show you the difference between the two.

Living by the sea opens up a whole new range of delicacies. Shell-fish, straight from the beach and still tasting of the sea. Mussels are a lucky find, but remember that only mussels off the rocks are safe for eating. Those attached to wooden groins or metal are risky, and you should check that there are no sewage outlets nearby. Other shellfish to hunt for are cockles, whelks, winkles, but again check that they are safe for eating. Standing one of the local fishermen a pint will probably supply all the information you need, and a lot more besides. A large shrimping net might be a good investment. A friend who lives on the Kent coast trails one of these along the beach, and boils up the catch – small fish, shrimps, baby crabs – into a good fish soup, bouillabaisse style, with lots of garlic and herbs, and a little cream.

Chatting up local farmers can also be helpful, and might produce an occasional hare, rabbit or pigeon, as well as odd things like buttermilk. Not for free, of course, but cheaper than shop prices.

French Dressing (Vinaigrette)

The most commonly used dressing for both cooked and raw salads, this is composed, in its classic state, of nothing but oil, vinegar, salt and pepper. Three parts oil, to one part vinegar, a good pinch of salt and pepper to taste.

Unless you are using the best quality ingredients, however – French wine vinegar, fine olive oil – the dressing will almost certainly be im-proved by adding various other flavourings. The choice is huge and there is nothing to stop you working out your own formula. But the usual garlic and mustard one, with or without chopped fresh herbs, is hard to beat. In this case you can use 1 crushed garlic clove and 1 tea-spoon French mustard (or a pinch of mustard powder) with the basic oil/vinegar mixture, and as many chopped herbs – chives, tarragon, parsley, thyme, chervil, basil are a few often used – as you like. About 1 teaspoon sugar is an improvement is you are using malt vinegar and powder mustard. If you like a suggestion of garlic more than the actual bulb, rub a cut clove round the salad bowl, or on a crust of stale bread, sprinkled with a few drops of oil, which you bury at the bottom of the salad, to exhale, as the French writers lyrically put it, its incomparable fragrance.

You can mix up the dressing in the salad bowl itself, stirring the various ingredients into the oil before adding the vinegar and chopped herbs. Or, more economically, you can shake it up in a bottle or screw-topped jar. Whichever way, make sure the ingredients are well mixed before dressing the salad, and toss the salad with a couple of spoons (less fastidious people can use their fingers) until it is all well coated. Once dressed, try not to leave the salad standing too long – this applies to lettuce, cress, chicory and curly endive in particular – or it will begin to go flabby and the oil and vinegar will separate.

Other ingredients which turn up in salad dressings include grated orange rind, crumbled blue cheese (an American fad this), a whole range of fancy vinegars – cider, tarragon, garlic – honey, nuts, sultanas, white wine, Tabasco, Worcestershire sauce, lemon juice, sieved hard-boiled egg yolk, pounded anchovies. Also more exotic herbs, like fennel and dill. There is no harm in experimenting a little, though I would not advise trying them all out at once.

 ## Mayonnaise

Mayonnaise seems to share with soufflés an undeserved reputation for being as unpredictable as an operatic diva. I can't really see it myself. It can, and occasionally does, curdle, for no very clear reason, but it can almost always be rescued by starting again with a fresh egg yolk and beating in the curdled substance little by little. Make sure all the ingredients are at room temperature. Remove eggs from the fridge or cool larder in advance. It is also a good idea to preheat the jug for the oil by rinsing with boiling water, then drying, before filling with oil.

For a smallish quantity of mayonnaise, allow one egg yolk to approximately 300 ml (½ pint) olive oil. *Do* use real olive oil. The flavour of the oil is the whole point of the sauce.

To make it, you need a bowl, a wooden spoon, a small jug for the oil, a little mustard powder, salt and pepper to mix in to the egg yolk, and a little vinegar or a squeeze of lemon juice to finish off with.

Break the yolk into the bowl. Stir well with your spoon, blending in the dry ingredients until smooth. Now start adding the oil, a drop or two at a time, stirring between each addition. After a minute or so the mixture in the bowl should be getting the smooth, shiny look and firm consistency of a successful oil-and-egg-yolk emulsion, which is what a mayonnaise is. When it gets to this stage you can step up the oil doses a little – a drip instead of a drop, but make sure you stir it in thoroughly before adding more. By the time you have used up more than half the oil, you can increase this to a small splash. When your oil allowance is gone, you should have a firm, pale yellow substance, rather similar to a packet custard in consistency. A squeeze of lemon juice or a dash of vinegar stirred in rapidly will thin it down. If it still seems too firm, you can add more oil, or a little boiling water (about 1 tablespoon) to lighten it, though personally I think a rather solid mayonnaise has more pungency. The sauce is now ready to be mixed into salads, or used to coat hard-boiled eggs, cold fish, chicken, and so forth.

When your mayonnaise curdles, you will be confronted by a queasy mixture with a runny texture which refuses to jell as a mayonnaise should. If you are in any doubt, leave the mixture to stand for a few minutes – if it *has* curdled, or separated, one look will confirm the fact. What you do now is break another egg yolk into a fresh bowl, add the usual ingredients, stir in the oil, drop by drop, until firm and only then add your curdled mixture, little by little, alternating with oil. The only snag to this is that you will need to use more oil to get the consistency right, so you will have more mayonnaise at the end. The surplus can be stored in the fridge for a few days in a glass jar with a screw top.

Basic mayonnaise can be converted into various other classic sauces by adding certain ingredients. Sauce Rémoulade, for instance, a sharp sauce which is delicious with grilled meat, is plain mayonnaise (300 ml/½ pint) with rather more mustard added (2 teaspoons) plus some chopped gherkins and capers, a dash of anchovy essence and a spoonful of chopped herbs, in this case parsley, tarragon and chervil. (If you can't get them all never mind.)

The celebrated Sauce Tartare, which is excellent with rather fattier, fried food (fish, chops, etc.), has 1 hard-boiled egg yolk worked into the raw egg yolk before proceeding as for mayonnaise. At the end, add rather more vinegar and chopped gherkins, capers and herbs as for Rémoulade, plus the chopped white of the hard-boiled egg.

 ## Aïoli

Aïoli is a mayonnaise powerfully flavoured with garlic. In Provence, where it comes from, they eat it with plainly boiled fish or beef and an assortment of vegetables – carrots, beans, potatoes – also boiled and usually hot. It also goes well with hard-boiled eggs, and boiled chicken. If you like garlic, you will probably find yourself thinking up excuses for eating aïoli.

Start by pounding two or three cloves of garlic (3 garlic cloves, 1 egg yolk and 500 ml/18 fl oz oil is about right for four people) to a pulp, then stir in the egg yolk and add the oil drop by drop to start with, beating all the time with a wooden spoon. When it starts to thicken, you can add the oil in slightly larger quantities. The procedure, in other words, is exactly as for mayonnaise. (See above for what to do if it should curdle.) When you have made as much as you need, add a squeeze of lemon juice and a little salt, and stir again. This yields a stiff, almost solid yellow emulsion, which can be extended with tepid water to soften the taste and make a more fluid sauce. Up to a third of the mayonnaise volume is fine. Add a little at a time, beating until smooth.

Try this with boiled cod steaks, and an assortment of vegetables.

Bread Sauce

Bread sauce and Cumberland sauce are Britain's most distinguished creations in the sauce line. Even the French, who like to damn our cooking with the faintest of praise, are impressed by these two. Bread sauce, as you doubtless know, is eaten with roast chicken. Even if you don't have roast chicken very often, the sauce is worth knowing about because it is easily made and always popular.

2 cloves	3-4 tablespoons fresh white
1 medium onion	breadcrumbs
1 bay leaf	a little butter or cream
300 ml (½ pint) milk	salt and pepper

Stick the cloves into the onion and put this and the bay leaf with the milk in a saucepan. Cover and set on a very low heat for 10–20 minutes or until the milk is well flavoured. Take out the onion and bay leaf, stir in the crumbs and simmer for a few minutes or until the sauce is thick but not stodgy. Season with salt and pepper and add a little butter (or cream if you have any to spare). Heat through and serve.

Basic White Sauce

Basic white sauce, like basic stock, is a neutral-tasting compound which absorbs the flavours you add to it. I don't think there is much to be said for the practice of pouring it over boiled vegetables to make them look more genteel, but as a binding for certain casserole dishes – fish pie, onion, bacon and potato hotpot – and as a base for cheese and onion sauces, it is extremely useful. A thick white sauce is also the foundation for most soufflés.

For some reason, the making of this sauce is surrounded with complications in most cookbooks. The milk, they tell you, should be heated separately, added little by little to the flour-and-butter mixture, and the whole preparation needs constant stirring to prevent lumps or burning. The method suggested here, which was given to me by a wise and experienced cook, is beautifully simple, uses only one pan, and you don't even need to stir – though I must admit I usually do once or twice to be on the safe side. The whole operation only takes three or four minutes.

MAKES 600 ML/1 PINT

15 g (½ oz) butter   600 ml (1 pint) milk
1 heaped tablespoon plain flour

Melt the butter in a saucepan over a moderate heat, stir in the flour thoroughly, pour in the milk (cold), increase the heat and bring fairly rapidly to the boil. I usually give it a stir at this point to make sure it is not sticking to the bottom of the pan, though if you don't cook it over fierce heat it shouldn't do so. In a few minutes it will have thickened to the right consistency. If there are any lumps you can disperse them with a few turns of the rotary whisk.

If you are using the white sauce as a base for cheese or onion sauce, you should simmer it gently for a while to get rid of the taste of the flour. Twenty minutes, over an asbestos mat, would be ideal, but 10 minutes is adequate. If it is to be used in a dish which requires further cooking anyway, like fish pie, you can dispense with the extra simmering and it will be ready as soon as it has thickened.

Green Sauce

A sharp, pungent sauce to serve with fish, and fatty meats like pork chops.

1 slice of white bread, crusts removed   2 anchovies
1 tablespoon wine vinegar   olive oil
1 garlic clove, roughly chopped   black pepper
2 teaspoons capers, drained

Soak the bread in the vinegar. Pound the garlic with the capers and anchovies in a mortar or in a strong bowl with the end of a rolling pin. Squeeze the vinegar out of the bread and add it to the mortar or bowl with the parsley. Pound again, then stir in enough olive oil to make a thick sauce. Add pepper to taste.

Agresto

This Italian pasta sauce can be made with any nuts you have, including those cocktail packets of 'mixed nuts'. The only nuts I think are really unsuitable are peanuts, which would give the sauce too oriental a

173

flavour, and pistachios which are prohibitively expensive. It's a reliable store-cupboard stand-by.

1 lemon	*2 garlic cloves*
50 g (2 oz) walnuts or hazelnuts	*a pinch of sugar*
50 g (2 oz) almonds	*black pepper*
1 thick slice of white bread	
1 sprig of fresh parsley, finely chopped	

Wash the lemon vigorously to rid it of sprays and wax, then grate the rind from the skin, being careful not to include any pith, and squeeze out the juice. Remove the skin from the nuts by covering them in boiling water for a couple of minutes, then rubbing the skins off in a tea-towel.

In a mortar, blender or food processor, blend the nuts together with the garlic, lemon juice and rind, and when it's a paste add the bread, parsley and sugar. Continue to blend until it's smooth. Heat the mixture gently in a small heavy-based saucepan, adding enough water to give it a more sauce-like consistency, but do not let it boil. Season generously with black pepper. Serve it more or less diluted depending on the shape of your pasta and quite thick if it is to be a sauce to go with poultry, game or beef.

Garlic Purée

a whole string of garlic bulbs	*salt*
olive oil	

Wrap the unpeeled heads of garlic together in kitchen foil and cook in the oven at 190°C (375°F) mark 5 for 1 hour. Leave them to cool, then unwrap them and skin them. Press the cloves through a sieve, cover with olive oil and keep in a jar in the fridge. Add to sauces, pasta or stuffings, or use to rub on meat or fish for grilling or roasting.

Aubergine Purée

3 aubergines	*2-3 tablespoons chopped fresh parsley*
1-2 garlic cloves, crushed	*or coriander*
3 tablespoons olive oil	*salt and black pepper*
juice of 1 lemon	*1 teaspoon paprika*

Char the aubergines under the grill or over a gas ring, or place them in the oven at 230°C (450°F) mark 8 until they soften. Peel the aubergines, squeeze out the excess juice and pound them with the garlic in a mortar or blender. Mix in the oil gradually, then the lemon juice, herbs and salt, pepper and paprika. Serve as a dip for pitta bread.

Pauper's Pesto

4 SERVINGS

50 g (2 oz) almonds
3 garlic cloves
a large bunch of fresh parsley and/or
    other herbs
50 g (2 oz) Pecorino cheese (or
    Parmesan, but Pecorino is
    cheaper)

5 tablespoons olive oil
salt and black pepper

In a pestle and mortar, crush the nuts with the garlic cloves. Tear up the herbs and crush these along with the nuts and garlic. Grate the cheese into it, pour over the oil, season with black pepper and a little salt and pour over freshly cooked pasta.

Mint and Yogurt Dip

Local Bangladeshi restaurants serve this to dip onion bhajis in, but lately I have noticed it migrating to city wine bars, as one of various dips for crudités. It is an absolute cheat but simple and refreshing.

150 g (5 oz) carton of natural yogurt
2-3 tablespoons bottled mint sauce or
    jelly

a little fresh coriander, finely chopped
    (optional)

Mix all the ingredients together well in a bowl. You may like to add a little salt or lemon juice.

Onion Relish

Some startlingly simple ideas can make good eating. This primitive but tasty relish was dished up at a café in Lincoln with ham and eggs.

3 large onions, sliced quite
    thinly
1 tablespoon salt

a sprinkling of wine or cider vinegar
    and very finely chopped parsley,
    to serve

Salting the onions and leaving them overnight, or for a few hours, sweats the 'fire' out of them and makes them limp but juicy. Shake the onions with the salt. Rinse quickly in cold water to remove excess salt, and dry on absorbent paper. Serve with a sprinkling of vinegar and very finely chopped parsley.

Home-made Spiced Olives

This is a simple way to buzz up the flavour of those Greek olives preserved in brine and sold in plastic packs. Covering them with oil preserves them, herbs and spices improve their flavour, and as a bonus, the oil itself – a mixture of olive and sunflower or safflower – takes on an intensity of flavour which adds life to salad dressings, pasta, etc.

575 g (19 oz) pack of black olives in brine
2 teaspoons coriander seeds
1 teaspoon black peppercorns
2 large garlic cloves, unpeeled but crushed slightly

several dried red chillies
1 teaspoon salt
2-3 sprigs of fresh rosemary and thyme
olive and sunflower or safflower oil, to cover

Drain the olives in a colander or sieve. Heat the coriander seeds and peppercorns for a minute in a small frying pan to make them more aromatic, then bruise them in a pestle and mortar or in a strong bowl with the end of a rolling pin. Layer the olives, garlic and whole chillies, with a sprinkling of salt and the crushed spices, in a glass jar with a lid. Push the herb sprigs down the sides. Pour in enough of the mixed oils to cover the ingredients, seal the jar and store for a few days before eating. Rather than using the oil for cooking, you could simply replenish the jar with more olives.

Potted Cheese

Cheese should really be kept in a cold larder, rather than the fridge, but mostly it gets bunged into the latter and all of a sudden one is feeling guilty about waste, contemplating a rubble of dry hunks and heels of assorted cheese. Potting it, which means breaking it down in the processor to mix with soft butter and other seasonings, re-cycles the cheese scraps very satisfactorily, to eat with biscuits or on toast. Many people like potted cheese better than ordinary.

odds and ends of cheeses, hard or
   semi-hard
approx half the weight of cheese in
   softened butter
enough dry or made mustard to taste

salt and pepper
a splash of any spirits available –
   port, whisky, sherry, etc.
a splash of Worcestershire sauce
1/2 teaspoon cayenne pepper

Cut the rinds off all the cheeses and process with all the other ingredients until smooth. Taste. You may need to add more of something; it rather depends on what cheeses you used. If you are eating it immediately, you can slurp ends of cream cartons in too, to give a 'spreading consistency'. Keep in the fridge.

Dandelion Salad

Young tender dandelion leaves make a tasty salad, either mixed up with the usual greenstuff, or on their own. If the dandelions are growing in your garden, you can make them more tender by laying a tile over the plant. With wild ones just take the youngest leaves, but pick them from a clean spot – not a roadside verge.

Dress either with Vinaigrette (see page 169) or this hot bacon dressing. De-rind a few rashers of bacon and cut them into cubes. Put them in a frying pan and cook over a moderate heat until the fat has melted a bit and the bacon pieces are crisp. Quickly stir 1 tablespoon vinegar into the pan and pour the whole lot over your salad.

N O T E : *This dressing also goes well with curly endive (frisée) and the coarser varieties of lettuce.*

Rillettes

A nice starter to eat with fresh bread, gherkins and a bowl of radishes.

6-8 SERVINGS
900 g (2 lb) belly or shoulder of
   pork, cut into narrow strips
250 ml (8 fl oz) water
2 cloves
2 bay leaves

chopped fresh thyme
2 garlic cloves, crushed
salt and pepper
quatre-épices

Put the pork in a heavy-based saucepan with the water, cloves, bay leaves and some thyme. Cover and cook over a very low heat for 4 hours. Alternatively, put the ingredients in a casserole, cover and cook in the oven at 140°C (275°F) mark 1 for 4 hours.

Pour the meat and fat through a sieve over a bowl and press the meat to extract as much fat as possible. Reserve the fat. Pound the meat in a pestle and mortar or in a strong bowl with the end of a rolling pin. Transfer the meat to a large bowl. Using two forks, pull the meat fibres apart, separating it into strands. Season with a little garlic, ground black pepper, quatre-épices and thyme, then return the meat to the pan and cook for a further 30 minutes without the fat.

Pack the meat tightly into several small sterilised pots. Spoon some of the fat from the first cooking from the top of the bowl, leaving any juices or jelly behind, and melt it once more. Pour it over the rillettes to a depth of 1 cm (½ inch). Cover the fat closely with a piece of foil or greaseproof paper, and tie a large piece over the top of each pot. The rillettes will keep in a cool place for 6 months.

Argentine Chorizo

My mother's family come from the Argentine, and this is the sort of sausage they made on the *estancia*, for drying out slowly in a warm kitchen. Beef is naturally included, and helps the drying process as it dries quicker than pork. Paprika provides the characteristic bright orange-red colour.

12-14 SERVINGS

2 kg (4 lb) belly of pork
½ nutmeg, grated
1 teaspoon ground cloves
½ bottle red wine (a Rioja or Portuguese Douro)
6 garlic cloves, crushed
3 tablespoons dried thyme, rosemary and oregano mixed

2-3 tablespoons paprika or pimenton (see Note)
3 tablespoons salt
½ tablespoon black peppercorns, crushed
1 kg (2 lb) shin of beef
pig casings

Strip the rind from the pork, cut out any bones, and cut off the thick outer layer of fat. Dice this and set aside. Grind the spices together in a mortar. Put the wine, garlic, ground spices and herbs in a saucepan and boil for 1-2 minutes. Add the paprika or pimenton, salt and crushed black peppercorns, then remove from the heat and leave to cool. Cut off as much gristle as possible from the beef, dice roughly with the leaner pork and then put through a coarse mincer. Pick out any stringy bits which eluded the mincer. Strain the marinade, and pour over the meats. Add the diced pork fat. Mix well with your hands and leave to stand overnight.

Next day, stuff the casings, making 15 cm (6 inch) links. Hang in a warm, dry place for 1-2 weeks, or until hard and knobbly, then transfer to a cool, dry place. As they dry out, the sausages will get smaller and harder, and need longer cooking. The flavour is magnificently concentrated; this is a sausage to add sparingly to stews and casseroles and bean dishes, or dice into piperade or a cabbage stuffing.

NOTE: *Pimenton, if you can get it, is a sweeter version of paprika and what chorizo would be made with. My mother used to get her ingredients in bulk and have them minced and stuffed into casings by her obliging butcher, a possibility worth exploring.*

Chicken Liver Pâté

6 SERVINGS

450 g (1 lb) chicken or turkey livers
125 g (4 oz) butter
2 garlic cloves (or more if you like),
    chopped
1 sprig of thyme, basil or marjoram

salt and pepper
100 ml (4 fl oz) sherry
100 ml (4 fl oz) brandy
50 g (2 oz) butter (optional)

Chop the livers, removing any greenish or discoloured bits carefully as these will give a bitter taste. Melt the butter in a heavy sauté or frying pan and put in the garlic. Let it soften just a little – don't allow it to brown. Put in the chicken livers and turn them about until they are firm and brown all over. Leaving them pink inside used to be recommended but with the risk of salmonella it's as well to cook them through.

Sprinkle over the finely chopped herbs. Spoon the chicken livers into a sieve over the serving dish (reserving the pan juices) and press through with a wooden spoon – you could use a food processor for this job if you have one, or if you like a coarser pâté, simply chop the livers up on a board (a large knife or mezzaluna is helpful for this). Season with a pinch of salt and plenty of black pepper. Pour the sherry and brandy into the hot pan, let it sizzle for a few moments, then stir the juices in with the livers. Let the mixture cool.

If you want it to keep for a few days, pour some melted butter over to seal it and keep it in the fridge. Eat with hot toast for a starter or with toast and salad as a supper or light lunch dish.

Mutton Ham

16-20 SERVINGS

a bunch of fresh herbs
a few peppercorns
a blade of mace
a leg of lamb
honey, to glaze

FOR THE MARINADE

125 g (4 oz) brown sugar
2 teaspoons ground cloves
1 teaspoon pepper
1 teaspoon ground mace
¼ teaspoon ground ginger
125 g (4 oz) salt

Mix together all the marinade ingredients, except the salt, and rub well into the lamb and down by the bone. Let it stand for a few hours and then rub in the salt. Place in a large dish and leave to stand for six days, turning the joint twice a day and spooning the juices over it assiduously.

To cook the lamb, soak the joint in water for a few hours, then place in lukewarm water in a large saucepan to which you have added a bunch of herbs, some peppercorns, and a blade of mace.

Bring to the boil, then reduce the heat and cook slowly until tender, allowing 25 minutes per 450 g (1 lb), plus 25 minutes. Just before serving, glaze the joint by brushing it with honey (dissolved in a little boiling water if it's very thick). Serve hot.

Fleur Kelly's Roman Loaf

Fresco artist Fleur Kelly bakes a huge loaf two or three times a week in her Aga. It tastes the way bread should – dense, springy, and full of flavour. A slice with pâté, cheese or, on one occasion, a bowl of baby beetroot with mayonnaise, is a meal in itself. The ample rounded shape was inspired by loaves in the Roman frescoes Fleur copies to hang on her walls. Unlike most bread doughs, this one requires no kneading, and only one long rising. Fleur goes to some trouble to find a special unbleached strong white flour, supplied by a local West Country miller, but a similar one is also available in supermarkets.

MAKES 1 LARGE LOAF

1.4-1.8 kg (3-4 lb) unbleached
   strong white flour
1 sachet fast action dried yeast

1 tablespoon salt
1 tablespoon sugar

Mix together all the ingredients in a very large (9 litre/2 gallon) bowl.

Add enough warm water to make a loose, sticky mixture. Stir the mixture rapidly with your hand, just enough to combine the ingredients. Cover the bowl with a clean, damp cloth and leave to rise overnight, or even until the following lunchtime, in the warm near the Aga. The next morning, give the mixture a quick scoop round with your hand, then turn it on to a baking sheet sprinkled with flour. Put it in the bottom of the Aga's top oven for 45-60 minutes, or until the crust is firm and the loaf feels springy. Stand the loaf up sideways after taking it from the oven, or the base is liable to become soggy.

VARIATION: Sprinkle a handful of sesame or poppy seeds over the loaf after the first 30 minutes of cooking.

Soda Bread

This traditional Irish bread, made without yeast, is a useful standby for holidays, and other times when bread supplies might run out. A handful of currants or sultanas added to the dough makes a nice teabread, eaten with butter, hot from the oven. Ideally the bread should be made with buttermilk.

MAKES 1 LOAF
450 g (1 lb) plain flour
1 teaspoon salt
1 teaspoon bicarbonate of soda

1 teaspoon sugar (optional)
buttermilk

Sift the dry ingredients together into a bowl. Make a well in the centre and gradually add the buttermilk, little by little, stirring in the flour until you have a soft dough and the bowl is fairly clean. Turn the dough on to a floured surface and knead lightly. Pat it into a round about 3 cm (1¼ inches) thick. Lay it on a lightly greased baking sheet and, using a sharp knife, make a cross-shaped cut in the centre. Bake on the middle shelf of the oven at 220°C (425°F) mark 7 for about 35 minutes. Remove the bread from the baking sheet and tap the bottom to make sure it is cooked thoroughly – it should sound hollow. Leave to cool or eat warm.

Caraway Tea Bread

A traditional feature of nursery teas, this is far too good to disappear along with nannies and starched tablecloths. Tea bread in this case means a plain cake which should be baked in a loaf tin, to be sliced and eaten with lots of butter. The caraway seeds – beloved of Victorian cookery – give it a unique flavour.

350 g (12 oz) strong white flour
2 teaspoons baking powder
175 g (6 oz) caster sugar
75 g (3 oz) butter

150 ml (¼ pint) boiling milk
1 egg, beaten
3 teaspoons ground caraway seeds

Sift the flour and baking powder twice, add the sugar and lightly rub in the butter or margarine. Mix scalded milk, which has been left to cool a little, with well beaten egg and ground caraway seeds. (To achieve the best flavour, lightly heat the seeds in a frying pan for a minute, then pound in a mortar or whizz in an electric coffee grinder.) Stir the milk and egg mixture into the dry ingredients, beat until well mixed, turn on to a floured board and knead quickly into a loaf tin measuring about 20 × 10 cm (8 × 4 inches). Bake on the middle shelf of the oven at 190°C (375°F) mark 5 for 1 hour or until it feels firm on top. Cover the top with buttered paper to prevent scorching, if necessary.

Cinnamon Biscuits

The cinnamon gives these biscuits a pleasant, not-too-sweet flavour, more popular with adults than children.

MAKES 24
75 g (3 oz) butter, softened
75 g (3 oz) caster sugar
1 teaspoon ground cinnamon

175 g (6 oz) plain flour
1 egg, beaten

Cream the butter and sugar together. Sift together the cinnamon and flour and gradually beat it into the creamed butter and sugar. Finally, add the beaten egg and mix it all together to a stiff paste. Roll out on a floured surface and cut into rounds with a cutter or glass. Lay these on a lightly oiled baking sheet and bake in the oven at 180°C (350°F) mark 4 for about 30 minutes or until crisp.

Oatcakes

Useful when you run out of bread as they are quick to make. Oatcakes freeze well.

MAKES 30

175 g (6 oz) fine or medium oatmeal (not porridge oats)
50 g (2 oz) plain flour
½ teaspoon salt

¼ teaspoon bicarbonate of soda
40 g (1½ oz) butter, margarine or lard
2 tablespoons boiling water

Mix the dry ingredients (oatmeal, flour, salt and soda) together in a bowl. Melt the fat in boiling water, add it to the dry mixture and knead lightly (adding a drop more water if needed to give a firm dough). Roll out thinly on a surface floured with a handful of oatmeal and cut it into triangles with a knife. Place on a greased baking sheet and bake in the oven at 200°C (400°F) mark 6 for 15 minutes or until crisp. Leave on a rack in a warm place to dry out.

Jam-making

The essential article for jam-making is a very large saucepan. Traditionally, these were made of copper, but an aluminium pan is just as satisfactory. It must be perfectly clean to prevent the sugar catching and burning. Where the recipe calls for warmed sugar, this means sugar which has been poured out into a large shallow baking tin and warmed in the oven for 10 minutes or so. The oven must be set at a low temperature (about 150°C/300°F/mark 2) so that the sugar does not actually melt. You can test when it is warmed by sticking your finger in. The idea of this is to ensure that the sugar melts almost instantly on contact with the hot fruit mixture.

Testing for setting is not, I must admit, a magically simple process. The usual advice is to pour a little of the jam on to a saucer, and put it in

183

the fridge or outside the window to cool off for a few minutes. If the jam is going to set, the stuff in the saucer will have formed a slight skin which wrinkles when you blow on it. Unless the recipe specifically instructs you to stop cooking after a certain time, you may need to go on testing and boiling for rather longer than indicated. It all depends on the amount of pectin (natural setting agent) in the fruit, and this can vary with the age and quality of the fruit. When in doubt, though, it is often better to chance the jam being a little runny than to boil on grimly, as the sugar does tend to burn or thicken drastically after a certain point, and jam which has to be hacked out of its container with a stout blade is a mixed blessing. Boil, in the case of jams, means boil *hard*, unless otherwise indicated. The stuff is liable to spit and splutter, so approach it cautiously, and use a long-handled wooden spoon for stirring or testing.

Having delivered all these warnings, I would just like to add that making jam satisfies some streak of the alchemist in one, in a way most cookery does not. Filling up your row of little jars (they should all be thoroughly washed, dried and warmed in the oven) is a triumphant experience. If you are planning to keep any jams for a longish time, seal them carefully with the wax discs and cellophane tops sold for the purpose. Otherwise, I find screw-on lids are adequate.

Gooseberry Jam

Gooseberry jam is one of the easiest to make, as the fruit has a high pectin content and sets readily. If you like a slightly tart jam, it is also one of the nicest. Unripe gooseberries are best for jam as their skins are less tough.

MAKES 3.6-4.5 KG (8-10 LB)

1.8 kg (4 lb) under-ripe green gooseberries, topped and tailed

2.7 kg (6 lb) sugar, warmed
1.1 litres (2 pints) water

Put the gooseberries in a large saucepan with the water and bring slowly to the boil. Mash the berries with a spoon and cook for 20 minutes. Add the sugar and allow it to dissolve, then bring the jam to the boil and boil for 10 minutes. Test for setting by dropping a little jam on a cold saucer and putting it in a cool place for a minute or two. If setting point has been reached, the jam on the saucer will form a slight skin which will wrinkle when you blow on it or push your finger through it. You may need to go on boiling the jam for 15–20 minutes to reach setting point.

N O T E : *If you can cook the gooseberries in a copper preserving pan they will keep their green colour. Otherwise they will turn a pinkish-amber shade.*

Bramble Cheese

This has more texture than bramble jelly, but without the seed you find in bramble jams.

*equal quantities of blackberries and   granulated sugar
   cooking apples*

Wash the berries. Peel but do not core the apples and cut them up roughly. Put the fruit in a saucepan with water almost to cover and cook slowly, covered, until reduced to a pulp. Rub through a coarse sieve, adding a little more boiling water. Weigh the strained pulp and to each 450 g (1 lb), add 450 g (1 lb) sugar.

Warm gently, stirring, until the sugar has dissolved, then bring to the boil and boil until setting point is reached. Test (see above) after only a few minutes as this preserve reaches setting point very quickly.

Pot and seal in the usual way.

Seville Orange Marmalade

This is a coarse-cut, bitter marmalade.

MAKES ABOUT 1.4 KG (3 LB)
*450 g (1 lb) Seville oranges   900 g (2 lb) sugar, warmed
1.1 litres (2 pints) water*

Wash the oranges and put them in a saucepan with the water. Cover and simmer slowly for about 1½ hours, or until a blunt wooden skewer pierces the orange skin easily. Take the oranges out of the liquid, let them cool and then cut them up into small thick strips, keeping all the pulp and juice which oozes out of them. Extract the pips, put them in the liquid in the pan and boil steadily for 10 minutes to extract the pectin. Remove the pips and put in the cut orange pulp. Bring to the boil, and stir in the sugar. Remove the pan from the heat and go on stirring until all the sugar is dissolved. Return to the heat and boil rapidly until the marmalade reaches setting point. This may not take very long, so, to be on the safe side, start testing (see above) after 15 minutes. Pot and seal in the usual way.

Orange Marmalade

A medium-sweet marmalade.

MAKES ABOUT 2.3 KG (5 LB)

450g (1 lb) Seville or bitter oranges *1.4 kg (3 lb) sugar, warmed*
1.7 litres (3 pints) water *juice of 1 lemon*

Cut or mince the oranges finely, removing the pips. Tie the pips in a small piece of muslin. Soak the peel and pulp overnight in the water, together with the pips.

The next day, put the fruit, water and pips in a saucepan, cover and simmer slowly for about 1½ hours or until the peel is quite soft. Remove the bag of pips and stir in the sugar and lemon juice. Bring to the boil and boil rapidly for about 20 minutes or until setting point is reached (see page 183).

Dumpsideary Jam

A traditional English country jam, made with mixed orchard fruit – apples, plums, pears – which are ripe at the same time. The Irish version, 'Mixty Maxty', is much the same except that it omits the spices.

MAKES ABOUT 2.5-3.2 KG (5½-7 LB)

1 kg (2 lb) green cooking apples *grated rind and juice of 2 lemons*
1 kg (2 lb) pears *6 cloves*
1 kg (2 lb) plums *1 small cinnamon stick*
600 ml (1 pint) water *4.5 kg (9 lb) sugar*

Quarter the apples, slicing off the core and any brown parts. Do not peel. Chop the pears somewhat smaller, also removing soft or brown parts. Put them all, with the whole plums, into a large pan, with the water and cook gently and slowly until the flesh is all soft. Turn into a large nylon sieve, and rub through into a preserving pan. Keep some of the plum stones, cracking them with a hammer to extract the kernels. Weigh the pulp and warm the sugar. Add the grated lemon rind and lemon juice to the fruit. Tie bruised spices in a muslin bag and add. Stir in the warmed sugar, set over a moderate heat, stirring until the sugar melts, then boil rapidly, stirring often, until it reaches setting point (see page 183). Stir in the plum kernels, pot and cover.

Index

Acknowledgements

The author and publishers would like to thank the following for permission to reproduce adaptations of recipes:
Chatto & Windus for Seafood Dumplings, page 141 (from *The Pleasures of Cookery*, Frances Bissell); Pavilion Books for Green Beans Szechuan-style, page 145 (published as Green Beans with Chilli, in *The Taste of China*, Ken Hom) and for Flammeküche, page 144 (from *A Taste of Alsace*, Sue Style).

If you have enjoyed the *New Pauper's Cookbook*,
you may be interested in the

Oxfam Vegetarian Cookbook

COMPILED BY ROSE ELLIOT (£8.99)

To obtain your copy, simply telephone
Murlyn Services on:

0279 427203

Your copy will be dispatched to you
without delay, postage and packing free.
You may pay by cheque/postal order/VISA and should
allow 28 days for delivery.